SHRUBS, BUSHES & SMALL TREES

LESLIE JOHNS

TREASURE PRESS

Contents

4 INTRODUCTION

6 HOW TO USE TREES AND SHRUBS IN THE GARDEN

20 FACTORS DETERMINING WHAT PLANTS CAN BE GROWN

36 PLANT STOCK

42 SPECIAL QUALITIES

50 SMALL TREES

58 CONIFERS

62 EVERGREEN SHRUBS

76 DECIDUOUS SHRUBS

86 PLANTS FOR HEDGING

92 CLIMBERS

95 INDEX

Illustrations by
Chris Forsey: 16, 25, 28, 29, 33, 37, 48, 49, 80, 81, 84, 85, 92, 93
Ed Roberts: 5, 8, 9, 12-13, 20, 21, 44-45, 52-53, 56, 57, 64, 65, 68, 69, 72, 73, 76, 77, 89

Acknowledgements
The following photographs were especially taken for Octopus Books: Michael Boys 46, 50, 51, 59, 67, 71, 75, 79 top, 83, 87; Jerry Harpur 6-7, 14-15, 23 top, 43, 55, 63 below, 66, 74; Neil Holmes 23 below, 46-7; George Wright 19, 30-1, 63 top, 82, 90-1, 94.
The publishers also acknowledge the help of: Harry Smith Horticultural Photographic Collection 79 below.

First published in Great Britain in 1984 by Octopus Books Limited

This edition published in 1986 by
Treasure Press
59 Grosvenor Street
London W1

ISBN 1 85051 148 9

Printed in Hong Kong

INTRODUCTION

Shrubs and trees are the long-term residents of the garden. Usually planted as small, young specimens (although some can be grown from seed), they are placed in the positions they will continue to occupy for at least ten years, sometimes many more. Shrubs and trees can be grown for their flowers (rhododendrons, flowering cherries) or their foliage (maples), but the emphasis can also be on berries or other fruits (cotoneaster) or even on the bark colour (birch). Shrubs and trees lose their leaves each winter, in which case they are known as deciduous, or remain clothed all the year (evergreen), though in the latter case it would be more true to say that instead of the dramatic total loss of all leaves in the colder months, evergreens lose and renew their leaves slowly and regularly throughout the entire year.

One group of evergreen trees and shrubs which stands on its own is known as conifers because they are cone bearing. Although called evergreen, conifers can be green, grey, silver, gold or a glaucous blue-green. The flowers they bear are not apparent except to the experienced, but conifers can play a highly useful role in the garden because of their versatility.

Conifers can be ground-hugging, which means that they can be used as weed suppressors or to cover and conceal such ugly necessities as manhole covers. They can grow as a ball, as a dignified and perfectly shaped cone, or leap upwards as with the aptly named *Juniperus virginiana* 'Skyrocket'.

There is the widest possible choice among the trees and shrubs suitable for the garden and by careful and intelligent selection it is possible to use them, not only to give stability and permanence to the garden scene, but to pinpoint, emphasize or display the special, colourful virtues of the herbaceous material. They are undemanding in their care, and once they have been carefully and correctly planted they will seldom require major attention over a period of years.

Shrubs and bushes grow only on a short stem or branch directly from the soil surface. Trees can be bought or grown as standards, with a clean upright stem at least 1.5m (5ft) long; as half standards with a stem of about 1.2m (4ft); or as bushes. They can be broad headed like an oak, pyramidal like many conifers, fastigiate or columnar, or weeping.

Many trees and shrubs have been given familiar names such as lilac and maple, but endearing though these names may be it is always best if possible to learn and use correct botanical nomenclature. There are many lilacs, for example, but only one *Syringa vulgaris* 'Maud Notcutt', many maples, only one *Acer platanoides*.

HOW TO USE TREES AND SHRUBS IN THE GARDEN

SHRUBS IN MIXED BORDERS Where space in a garden is limited or where a greater interest and wider perspective is sought than would normally be provided by the traditional border of perennial herbaceous material, the mixed shrub border supplies answers to almost every problem. The shrubs themselves give an air of permanence and at the same time cut the amount of work involved. The herbaceous plants and the flowering bulbs bring a wider range of shape, colour and texture to the scene. The herbaceous plants and some of the bulbs may need to be dug up, divided or replaced each year, but the shrubs need no attention other than a mulch around the roots and an occasional pruning to keep the overall area under control and to allow the flower colour to be seen.

Choosing shrubs for a mixed border of this kind is not simple. The selection must be of those species and varieties that will not grow too large or too quickly, will provide flower colour to blend naturally with the surrounding herbaceous plants, will have a long flowering period or will fulfil a role by

virtue of overall shape, colour, size or texture of the leaves.

It may be possible to buy certain container-grown shrubs from a garden centre which are more or less mature in size and this way the mixed border can spring ready-grown into existence. However, as a general rule, younger and less mature shrubs should be bought and planted and these sometimes fail to receive the attention they deserve in the mixed border. Because the total period of growth will be considerably extended, it is always helpful to use younger specimens. A further advantage of this operation is that planted young, the shrubs acclimatize themselves, settle down and grow well. If the borders appear somewhat sparse because of the immaturity of the shrubs, then it is a simple matter to fill the space which they will eventually occupy with some quick-growing hardy or half-hardy annuals or even to plunge into the soil of the bed some pot-grown plants such as pelargoniums and remove them again when the winter arrives. It is essential to leave correct space between shrubs in the initial planting rather than attempt to fill vacant space by planting them too closely together. This will only result in a border consisting of nothing but those shrubs.

A mixed shrub border can exploit the seasons, providing interest and colour at all times by the careful and tasteful selection of shrubby plants and herbaceous material which will develop and reach a peak according to a pre-planned pattern.

PLANTING SPECIMEN SUBJECTS No more flattering situation for a tree can exist than in a smooth, green lawn — a specimen standing in the centre of a vacant stage, the target for the admiration of all eyes. This being so, it is obviously important that the tree or shrub should be chosen with care so that it is worthy of the attention it will receive.

Ask yourself a series of questions. Is the lawn large or small? Should the newly planted subject be in the centre, to one side, in the front or in the back? What sort of background will it receive? Will it be seen from the house? Will it be in the way of a path? Will it be an inconvenience when mowing? Should it be tall or spreading, evergreen or deciduous, green or other coloured, quite alone or with a little bed at its feet to hide the sometimes unattractive base?

When these and one or two more questions are answered you will already be halfway to choosing the right tree or shrub for the site. But do spend time and care on selection and bear the following points in mind. The subject chosen will last a decade, possibly the whole of your life or your period of residence in that house, so make sure you won't become bored with it. Will it present an attractive appearance in summer and winter and preferably have some peak of appearance or performance to which you can look forward year after year? Remember that it will grow and what looks delightful and happily in proportion when young and immature may be inconvenient, even ugly when fully grown and occupying far too much space in the lawn.

Whether to choose a small tree, evergreen or deciduous, a

Magnolia stellata

Betula pendula 'Youngii'

low-growing shrub or a conifer will depend not only on personal taste but on area and surroundings. The following brief list of possible plants will serve as suggestions and an introduction to the wide choice.

Trees include: *Betula pendula* 'Youngii', weeping form of the silver birch, grows up to 3m (10ft); *Parrotia persica*, large green leaves which turn gold, orange and red, grows up to 5m (16ft); *Fagus sylvatica* 'Dawick', slim, upright, gold leaves in autumn, up to 6m (19ft); *Liriodendron tulipifera*, the tulip tree, unusual shaped leaves gold in autumn, quick growing to 10m (33ft); *Robinia pseudoacacia* 'Frisia', bright yellow foliage, quick growing to 5m (16ft).

Shrubs: *Carpenteria californica*, evergreen with large white flowers, grows to 2m (6ft); *Cornus kousa chinensis*, masses of white flowers and large leaves turning brown gold in autumn, 2m (6ft); *Salix alba* 'Chermesina', narrow, upright, with pale green leaves and scarlet stems in winter, 2m (6ft). Among the conifers, have a look at *Chamaecyparis nootkatensis* 'Pendula', *Metasequoia glyptostroboides* and *Taxus baccata* 'Fastigiata', all fascinating and much more beautiful than their names.

SCREENS AND WINDBREAKS A hedge or a windbreak is more than a mere screen designed to divide one part of the garden from another or to provide dappled shade and a degree of privacy. A hedge is normally intended to keep people and animals out or in, and a windbreak must so stop, filter and subdue gales as to render them safe for plants and tolerable for humans. A double row of strong plants is essential for an effective barrier and these should grow from a deep and well-prepared trench. Stagger the plants and adhere to recommended planting distances.

There are many more types of hedges than are generally seen in most gardens. Many trees and shrubs can be adapted to make a barrier with a certain amount of pruning or clipping. Hedges can be low or tall, a light barrier or quite impenetrable, flowering or foliage, and it depends on your choice as to which materials you use, although it is wise to appreciate that some less well-known hedging materials may make excessive demands on the gardener or occupy too much space.

Subjects for traditional hedges, easily grown and managed, include several conifers such as cupressocyparis, cupressus, pinus, thuja and yew. Other materials often used are quickthorn, privet, green and purple beech, hornbeam, myrobalan plum and the field maple, *Acer campestre*.

If you like the idea of a flowering hedge you can consider roses, choosing species roses rather than specimen tea or multi-flowered types. If you have space, rhododendrons make a good thick hedge, including the tough *R. ponticum*. Several of the berberis family make excellent and almost impenetrable hedges, their sharp spines fulfilling one function while their flowers, foliage or berries satisfy a taste for colour. One or two cotoneasters and pyracanthas also provide both flowers and berries, while the attractive and popular *Prunus pissardi* 'Nigra' gives colour in the form of a deep purple foliage and masses of pink flowers each spring.

A good hedge is worth looking after, so ensure plenty of water at the roots in dry spells, give a light feed of general purpose fertilizer each spring, trim at least once a year, shaping to avoid accumulations of snow on top, if this is a problem, and for the first year or two keep weeds clear of the base.

Try to encourage growth at the base instead of at the top of the new hedge for the first year or two and do this by leaving the young shoots at the top and cutting back on those lower down. In many cases it is helpful to cut back the entire growth of a deciduous hedge to within 30cm (12in) of the ground soon after planting. This will encourage strong root growth and the development of a quantity of young shoots. A hornbeam or beech hedge should ideally not be pruned in any way for its first two years and hedges of practically all materials should be allowed to grow to their final required height before any trimming takes place at the top. Then aim to trim this a little slimmer than the width at the base.

Fagus sylvatica
Chamaecyparis lawsoniana

SHRUBS AS GROUND COVER The idea of planting low-growing shrubs to serve as a ground cover and cut out the chore of weeding is an attractive one and usually effective so long as the basic principles of ground-cover gardening are followed. It is essential to appreciate that ground-cover shrubs will not kill weeds already existing but will in time prevent weeds from growing under them. So in the early days when shrubs are planted at, say, 30cm (12in) intervals, the weeds will continue to grow for a year or two until the shrubs have grown and spread to cover the intervening spaces. Meanwhile the weeding will have to go on as before. Once the ground cover is established, it will not only suppress weeds but it will also prevent the sun from drying out the soil and heavy rain from scouring the site.

This being so, it is obviously helpful to use plants that will grow quickly and cover the ground thickly to suppress the weed growth. Perhaps the best subject for this purpose is ivy, available in several forms and colours. This produces many roots from its creeping stems and will soon make an impenetrable mat on the ground which will stop any normal weeds from growing through it. Similar to their speed of growth are the two periwinkles, lesser and greater, both of which bear small blue flowers in the spring. The well-known Rose of Sharon (*Hypericum calycinum*) is another flowering, low-growing plant which will quickly cover an area in need of

Juniperus sabina (left) and *Hypericum calycinum*

weed control treatment with its mass of yellow flowers.

The subjects to be used as ground cover will depend to some extent on the site. The materials mentioned above would not be attractive if used on a large scale, for they would look monotonous and dull. They should be employed in smaller areas which they will quickly cover. On the other hand, a striking, interesting and attractive space of considerable size can result from the use of selected varieties of ericas or heathers. Some of these may demand an acid soil, but many will grow well and spread effectively in ordinary soils, providing both flowers and foliage colour of remarkable depth and intensity. Ericas look particularly effective in weed-smothering beds when interspersed with dwarf and low-growing conifers in green, blue, gold or grey.

There are a number of low-growing shrubs that are successful and attractive as weed smotherers, but they are not all suitable to every type of soil and it is important to ask before ordering. Among these the following are to be recommended: *Epimedium perralderianum*, with glossy leaves and yellow flowers; *Mahonia aquifolium*, also called Oregon grape, for its purple berries; several varieties of cotoneaster, with bee-filled flowers and glossy red berries and particularly effective and attractive in paved or semi-paved areas; and almost any of the perfumed and flowering thymes, which creep over the stones and subdue all weeds trying to grow in the spaces.

WOODLAND GARDEN Where sufficient space is available, an informal woodland garden is a delightful feature. It is full of interest at all times of the year and once established it offers the gardener a charming way of merging the main, formal garden with the surrounding countryside. A woodland setting is particularly effective when viewed in conjunction with water; either a small natural lake or an artificial pond or stream set up specially for this purpose.

Cultivars (cultivated varieties) and native trees and shrubs can be grown side by side. For those keen on conservation, native trees and shrubs only can be grown to create a sanctuary and habitat for many kinds of wildlife. If you have existing woodland, it may need to be thinned; tall and spreading trees should be well spaced if other plants are to thrive beneath them. You should also aim for some open spaces where shrubs can spread themselves to their full limits and where special specimens can be placed to their best visual advantage.

Ordinary soils can accommodate a rich variety, ranging from, say, early flowering pussy willows, spring and summer blossom, to the glowing berried holly and the strawberry

fruited arbutus which so brighten mid-winter days. A good mixture of both evergreen and deciduous trees will thrive on acid soils to create a cover and a foil for brilliant azaleas and rhododendrons, camellias and other peat lovers. On limestone, beech, cherry, hawthorn, sorbus, larch and other conifers grow well and provide autumn hues.

The floor of the woodland can be closely carpeted with plants, shrubs, sub-shrubs such as periwinkle and herbaceous kinds, including those grown from bulbs. Ivies, which are extremely varied, are ideal for this purpose. The deep green leaved varieties will suit shady areas but the more colourful variegated ones should be given better light if they are to retain their colour. All of these will carpet as well as climb. The less shaded margins of the woodland and the borders of internal pathways can be planted with shrubs of varying height. The choice is almost limitless and can depend to a great extent upon your personal preferences. Shrubs and species roses, fuchsias, hydrangeas, choisya, berberis, pieris, phlomis and erica are all good examples. Here also climbers can be trained up trees.

TREES AND SHRUBS IN CONTAINERS It could be said that any plant which grows in the garden will also grow in a container, but in most cases this is only for a brief period and is dependent on the size of the plant and the container. At the same time this aspect of gardening presents opportunities too great to be ignored, for it means, for example, that in a garden composed of a limey soil it will still be possible to grow some of the lime-haters such as rhododendrons and azaleas by using a container filled with acid soil. It also means that a plant can be moved to suit the season, the occasion or even the whim of the moment.

The main problems encountered in container gardening are concerned with plant roots, for these are not only confined to a relatively small space but are completely divorced from the natural world, that great reservoir of soil of bottomless depth. Planted in the garden soil, any shrub during a hot, dry spell can send its roots far and wide and deep in search of moisture, but it cannot do this when planted in a container. It is therefore essential that container-grown plants should be watered thoroughly, sometimes as often as two or even three times a day. It is also vital that drainage is adequate, for where the drainage holes of a container become blocked and it fills with water, the plant or plants it holds will drown. So always ensure that the drainage holes are adequate for the size of container and see that the bottom 6-8cm (2-3in) of the container holds broken crocks, pebbles or some similar material to ensure swift and efficient drainage. When watering by hand the supply of moisture should be sufficient each time so that the water seeps or trickles from the drainage holes. This throughput of water is sure to leach much of the plant foods from the soil, so replace this by regular feeding and by top dressing with fresh compost.

Because any trees or shrubs grown in containers are already given star treatment by being selected for this attention, it is most effective to choose subjects which are restrained rather than colourful, architectural rather than flamboyant. *Fatsia japonica*, for example, is an evergreen shrub with large, palmate leaves on long stalks and milky white flowers late in the year. Several varieties of the New Zealand flax, *Phormium tenax*, with upright, sword-like leaves of different colours, are eminently suitable for container culture. *Convolvulus cneorum*, another evergreen, with its foliage covered in silvery hairs and white flowers in late summer, is always interesting in a restrained kind of way. A number of conifers — green, grey, gold and blue — of dwarf-growing varieties, can look most effective growing in containers and if the containers are large enough, a whole miniature garden can be created. You can choose types that will live for years in a trough or sink yet never grow to more than a metre (3ft) or so in height.

The choice of container is another important consideration. Not only must it suit the needs of the tree or shrub, but it should also complement the surrounding architecture.

WALL AND CLIMBING SHRUBS A good wall in the garden, whether high or low, particularly if it runs more or less north and south, can be of immense benefit, for it increases significantly the total area of the garden and it also permits the cultivation of certain plants, both ground growers and climbers, which would otherwise be impossible because of their tender nature. A south wall provides protection, attracts sun and gently releases absorbed warmth. A north wall gives protection and shade for more hardy or versatile plants.

Ground-growing plants can stand free of a wall and merely benefit from its protection, while others can lean against it and by means of its shelter climb up and along its face. You can also use low walls at the sides of steps or pathways for this purpose. Climbers can be divided into those that send out aerial roots which cling to the wall face and serve to pull up the new growth, those that cling by tendrils to any support provided such as trellis or support wires, and those that will climb only if tied in at regular intervals to supports of some kind. Even those climbers that attach themselves to a wall by means of aerial roots or sucker pads do little real harm to a sound wall and can be grown safely enough. Any damage is usually done by a vigorous climber such as a Virginia creeper or the rampant Russian vine *Polygonum baldschuanicum* that get their growing tips into cracks or crevices and then push their aggressive way in to enlarge the tiny space available. This allows in rain and frost so that in time the wall itself becomes damaged.

So long as a wary eye is kept on some climbers and over-enthusiasm curbed by cutting back too rampant growth, plants growing on or beside walls are relatively easy and certainly profitable to grow. But one or two elementary precautions must be taken. It will be noticed, for example, that the soil at the base of almost every wall is drier than that further away. This is due partly to the protection against rain given by the wall and partly to the fact that the wall's stone or brick tends to absorb any moisture available at its base. For these reasons it is helpful, if possible, to plant the roots of a wall climber not directly at the base of the wall but a small distance away and let the climbing shoots lean over to the wall. In time of drought pay special attention to wall climbers and give them additional water or a moisture-retentive mulch.

There is a tremendous range of materials for wall plants, ranging from roses, jasmine and honeysuckle through more utilitarian foliage climbers such as the invaluable ivies and the Virginia creeper with its brilliantly coloured leaves. There are productive grapes, quinces and even passion fruit, climbers with flowers of every hue and trailing plants with delicate and romantic perfumes, including a clematis to twine around your bedroom window with the evocative common name of 'The Fragrant Virgin's Bower', or less romantically, *Clematis flammula*.

Potentilla fruticosa 'Tangerine' will cascade over a brick wall in a prostrate manner covering the area as here beside some garden steps.

FACTORS DETERMINING WHAT PLANTS CAN BE GROWN

CLIMATE Weather is vital to the gardener, yet in no way can it be controlled. So on the basis that if you can't beat it, join it, it is wise to adapt your activities to take advantage of the climate. For example, if rain is imminent, this is the time to plant out seedlings or sow seed and if a hot, dry, windy day is forecast, weeds that are already hoed will die and disappear.

Plants can grow and flourish in heavy or persistent rains, but they die in drought. The most perilous time for all trees and shrubs is a period of drought when they have been newly planted. So conserve soil moisture by mulches and save as much rainwater as possible for use in dry periods. All plants are composed more of water in various forms than of any other substance and nearly all of this moisture is taken up by the plant through its roots.

Frost is considered to be an enemy of the gardener, and so indeed it can be if certain protective measures are not adopted, but it can also be a friend. Nothing is better than a heavy frost for breaking down clay into good, friable, easily worked earth. In winter always try to dig vacant ground and leave the soil in

Tie conifers in with twine to retain shape in heavy snowfalls.

great lumps or clods so that frost, rain and snow can break them down and reduce them to a crumbly texture.

We all know that frost cracks our water pipes because ice expands when it thaws. It does exactly the same thing with the tissues of some of our plants. If the rate of thaw after a frost can be slowed down, damage to the plants will be lessened. Take an early flowering camellia as an example. Plant it in a situation so that it is protected from the warmth of the early morning sun and instead let it thaw slowly in shade. On the other hand, frost can kill a young tree or shrub by depriving it of water. With soil moisture frozen, roots cannot absorb any.

Frosts tend to flow downhill. They will collect in a valley or a depression in the ground. If your land slopes, try to ensure that the lowest part is open and not blocked by a wall or hedge. This way frosts will roll down the garden and cause little or no damage on your land.

Young or newly planted trees and shrubs can be damaged or even killed by sharp frosts and by strong winds. Where this is the case a little protection can save them from both perils. It is possible to make a rough surround for a plant by inserting three or four lightweight stakes into the soil around the plant. Wind string around these to make a small enclosure. Roughly fill this with straw, dried bracken or even sheets of newspaper to keep out frosts and protect against winds. Do this carefully so as not to damage the spreading branches and twigs.

A plastic screen will protect young plants from the elements.

SUN AND SHADE Light is as vital to nearly all plants as is water, for light helps to create the organic matter of which the plant is made. Lack of light results in weak, spindly growth, pale or even white colouring, such as you get when chicory or dandelions are blanched by the exclusion of all light. Lack of light can kill a tree but is more likely in our gardens to lead to a weak or misshapen specimen, for the growth will tend to be in the direction of the strongest light.

Sunlight is also a source of heat and too much of both light and heat can be a danger to many plants, particularly trees and shrubs which have been newly planted and have a root system limited in extent. These roots provide the plant with moisture which is drawn up through the main trunk and its branches to the tiny twigs at the extremes and thus to the leaves, which exude the moisture. If the sun and warmth draw out this moisture, at a faster rate than it can be replaced, the plant will soon be in trouble, which is one reason why it is vital to ensure a sufficient supply of moisture to the roots of young plants. Some trees and shrubs will react to this dangerous water loss by drooping their leaves and others will move their leaves to an angle where the sun strikes less strongly on them. Once root growth is more mature and spreading most trees and shrubs have a better chance of looking after themselves. You can erect temporary screens in the interim while the plants mature: split-cane and greenhouse blinds make excellent screens.

Shortage of light rather than an excess is as a general rule more likely to be the problem in northern Europe. Gardening in a city can bring problems; not only is the quality of light poor because of polluted air, but its direct passage is often obstructed by high buildings. There are fortunately a number of trees and shrubs which will grow happily in shady conditions and it is well to have a look at some of these if you want to plant in difficult conditions of shade, remembering that when the shade is caused by larger trees and shrubs growing above the new planting, these will tend to absorb the major part of the existing plant foods from the soil, so special feeding programmes as well as watering may be necessary.

The laurels are good shrubs for shady conditions. The common laurel, *Prunus laurocerasus*, is a quick grower; the Portugual laurel, *Prunus lusitanica* and what is known as the Japanese laurel, *Aucuba japonica*, with its splendid golden-leaved varieties, are satisfactory subjects for the shade. All are evergreen. *Mahonia japonica bealei*, with its dainty sprays of yellow flowers, most camellias and the gorgeous winter-flowering laurustinus or *Viburnum tinus* will all grow well in shade.

Plants that like shade can also be used to landscape a shaded area of your garden which you might wish to use for just such a purpose. This is where shade-tolerant flowering shrubs and weeping subjects can make a perfect shady corner for sitting in on a hot summer day.

Pyracantha crenulata
Camellia japonica 'Apollo'

SOIL AND DRAINAGE All soil began as rock, pulverized through the ages to become no more suitable for plant growth than pure sand. It is the animal and vegetable matter in the soil, the decaying leaves, bones and waste matter of life, together with the bacteria that activate, enrich and re-texture it so that it becomes alive, nourishing and feeding the plants that grow in it. This organic matter, known as humus, is the most important element in all soils. It breaks down clay and makes it workable. It gives body to sand and enables it to absorb moisture. It invites air into the soil and holds moisture.

The humus in soil is used up where cultivation is intensive and therefore it is necessary to add to the soil constantly. Farmyard manure is a good source of humus, but equally valuable is homemade compost, which after all is no more than decayed vegetable matter of many kinds. Humus also provides the necessary conditions for bacterial activity. It helps to break down the soil into the basic chemicals which are then absorbed by the plant roots. It is helpful to plant growth for you to add these chemicals in the form of fertilizers. They are usually sold as a mixture of nitrogen (N), phosphates (P) and potash (K), often shown on the packet by the letters or by numbers only, indicating the relative proportions of each chemical. These fertilizers are obtainable as a granular or powder mixture or as a liquid. Dry mixtures must be watered into the soil. Apply according to the manufacturer's instructions – an extra dose may kill the plant.

It is possible to buy soils of various types, some tailored to specialized uses. A soil for cacti, for example, would contain a high proportion of coarse, sandy material to ensure the necessary sharp drainage. A soil for rhododendrons would be acid. The John Innes composts or soils, devised by the horticultural institute of that name, are blended to a strict formula, sterilized to kill dormant weed seeds and containing fertilizers of three strengths to suit seedlings, medium-sized plants and those that are mature.

Garden soil can vary widely in content, texture, acidity and alkalinity, richness and poverty and it is worth buying a small soil testing kit to discover any deficiencies in different parts of the garden so that these can be rectified. All soils tend to become more acidic as they are cultivated and although this can in some cases be of benefit, in others it can be a serious drawback to good and productive gardening.

Where a garden is created on low-lying land or on a heavy clay soil it can become boggy and wet. Unless a large area of land is involved, it is seldom necessary to go to the considerable trouble and expense of installing special drainage, for the problem can almost always be overcome over a period of cultivation by the addition of such materials as sharp sand and humus and simply by planting trees and shrubs that will absorb and use up most of the excess wet.

Various types of soil conditioners can be bought which are claimed to break down unworkable clay into friable soil and generally to improve the texture, productivity and drainage of problem soils. Some of these products, usually based on gypsum or on seaweed, can be helpful (though expensive) but none takes the place of the proper cultivation of the soil, planting it with suitable subjects and tending it regularly.

Make sure you understand the needs of a plant before you put it in its permanent position; for example, never plant willows near a house, a wall or near underground drains. Its far-reaching roots can cause damage in its search for moisture.

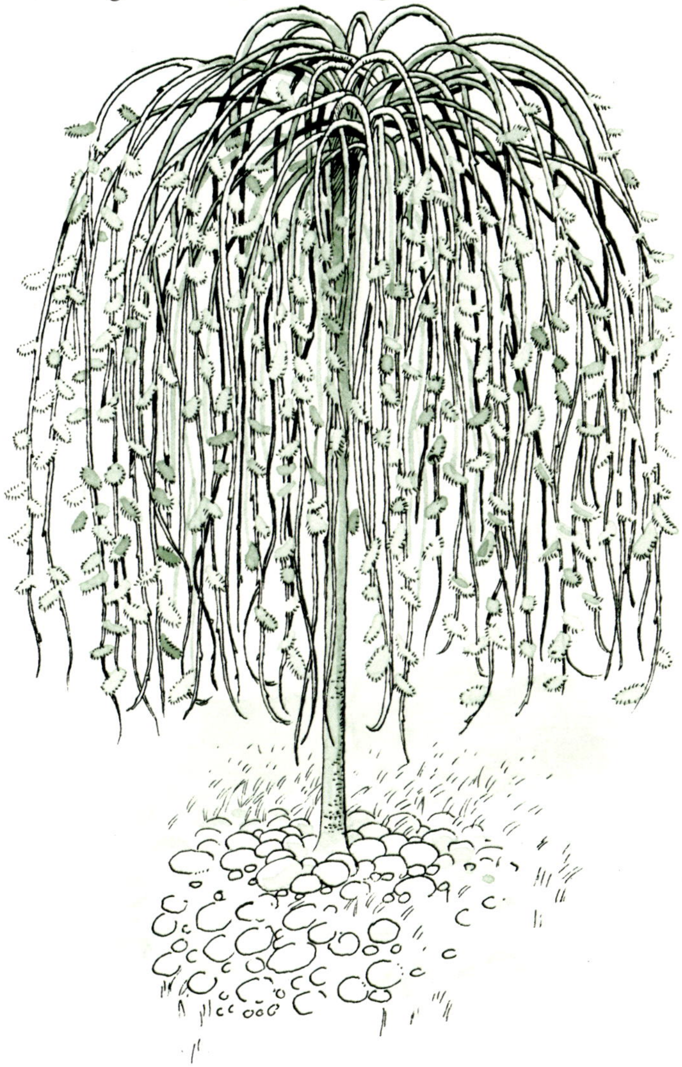

Salix caprea 'Pendula', the Kilmarnock willow which bears the pussy willow catkins. All willows thrive best in full sun and deep loamy soil.

WHEN AND HOW TO PLANT The trees and shrubs you buy can come in two forms, either dug from the nursery soil and delivered to you with bare roots usually wrapped with straw and hessian, or container grown, the roots still in a plastic pot of some sort. There is an important difference. The first must be dug from the soil and planted in your garden when the plant is dormant, during the winter months. Container-grown plants can go into the soil at any time of the year. More and more container-grown plants are being chosen because they can be seen growing with foliage and flowers.

Plant your bare root tree as soon as you can after receiving it so long as the weather is suitable, without frost or heavy rain. Dig a hole in the selected site, making it a little larger and deeper than the roots. While you are preparing the hole stand the young tree in a bucket of water for an hour or two to plump up the roots. Have ready some good planting soil, a mixture of some of the soil from the hole, some peat or homemade compost, a little coarse sand or perlite to improve the drainage and a handful of a gentle fertilizer such as bonemeal. If the tree looks top heavy and could be rocked by the wind, insert a strong stake before planting. Hammer it well into the soil in the base of the planting hole so that it stands firmly fixed and perpendicular. Then take the young tree or shrub and examine

1

2

the roots carefully, cutting away with secateurs any broken or damaged roots (1). Stand it in the planting hole and sift the soil gently over the roots, making sure that no air pockets are left (2). Firm the soil around the roots as you go and when the hole is half filled, tread the soil down with your foot. Continue adding the soil, making sure that when completed it will come exactly to the previous soil mark on the stem (3). Finish off by firming the soil down with your foot and leaving the plant standing in a slight saucer (see page 28). This aids watering in future (4).

Fix the tree to the stake, preferably using special tree ties, but otherwise use string, rope or some material such as an old nylon stocking, something that will hold firm without rubbing or chafing. Water the young tree thoroughly, sprinkling the foliage too if it is an evergreen and making quite sure that all the soil in the planting hole becomes moistened. Do not let this soil become dry for the first few months and examine the stake and tie when March winds begin to shake the plant in the soil.

To plant a container-grown tree follow exactly the same procedure except that when the plant is removed from its pot put the whole root ball into the planting hole, disturbing as little as possible. Try to firm the planting soil around the root ball to get much the same texture.

3

4

AFTERCARE The main beauty and benefit of growing trees and shrubs is that they demand little attention after they have been put into the soil. But some of these plants are expensive and deserve to be grown as well as possible to give a good return on your investment, so it is well to ensure that nothing goes wrong.

The importance of seeing that the newly planted shrub does not dry out has already been mentioned. Make sure that the whole plant, including all the leaves from tip to base, has been thoroughly wetted at each watering just as it would be by rain and unless you are quite sure that the soil is moist, give at least 10 litres (2 gallons) each time. It is helpful to apply a monthly all-over spray with foliar feed mixed to the manufacturer's instructions.

Keep the soil at the base of the plant free of weeds, but do not disturb the soil surface too vigorously as the young roots should be allowed to settle into the soil and grow rapidly. If weeds are removed by hand each time the plant is watered then the soil surface should remain clear and uncluttered. In particular avoid tap-rooted weeds such as dandelions and remove these completely including every piece of root while they are young.

Once the young plant has been in the soil for a couple of months and is obviously happy and doing well, it will normally be possible to ease off the watering programme. You can then kill several birds with one stone by applying a good mulch to the soil right around the plant. First make quite sure that the soil is moist, give it a good watering even when this does not really appear to be necessary. Then apply the mulch to the soil around the main stem. Do not allow it to touch the stem of the tree or shrub, but encircle it entirely. A bulky mulch such as farmyard manure or homemade compost can be up to 15cm (6in) deep and a mulch of peat or shredded bark about half this. If you have nothing else, grass mowings make an admirable mulch so long as the grass has not been treated recently with a hormone weedkiller.

A saucer-shaped basin beneath a newly planted shrub makes watering easier.

A mulch of this nature will do much to retain the moisture in the soil around the roots and at the same time keep them cool. The mulch will gradually disintegrate and disappear into the soil, enriching it and improving the texture. Worms and bacterial growth will be encouraged. Weed growth will be smothered almost completely and any weeds that do appear can be easily removed from the loose and open soil.

Remember that however well or thoroughly you mulch your new tree or shrub this is an activity designed to improve the soil structure rather than feed the plant, so in the early spring try to go around all your trees and give them each a handful of fertilizer. If this is powder or granular, sprinkle it in a circle about 30cm (12in) around the base and very lightly spike this in with a fork or hoe it into the top soil, being careful not to go too deep in case any roots are damaged.

With many trees and shrubs it is unnecessary to treat against pest and insect attack, but look carefully at your own materials each spring and see if there are signs of eaten leaves or other disfigurement and if so spray at once with an appropriate pesticide.

Compost bins can be bought ready for use. One such as this is ideal for the smaller garden. Enclosed compost heaps do not dry out quickly while the vegetable material decomposes. It takes about three months for compost to be ready for use.

PLANTING A HEDGE The technique of planting a hedge is exactly the same as that used for planting any normal tree or shrub except that you plant a series of them in a line, whether straight or curving. So instead of digging a single planting hole (see pages 26-7), or even a series of planting holes, the easiest way is to dig a trench along the required line. This must be wide enough to take a double row of shrubs, staggered, planted in effect at the top and bottom angles of a letter W. A single row may be suitable if you only want to provide a light screen.

To be effective your hedge must live for years in the same position. It should be clothed in foliage from top to bottom. It should look attractive in all seasons. It should grow quickly and evenly, but not so quickly that too much time has to be given to clipping or otherwise controlling.

First of all make sure that the soil in which the hedge is planted is rich and full of nourishment. If possible place a good layer of farmyard manure or similar material in the bottom of the trench into which the roots can grow and incorporate a handful of bonemeal or other slow-acting fertilizer into the planting soil.

To ensure foliage from ground level upwards it will be necessary to encourage new growth, so cut back the top of the

young trees or bushes by about a half soon after planting, but do no more trimming in the first year. In the second year let the hedge grow upwards and begin to trim the sides to get the required shape and to thicken up the growth in the vital centre. Do this two, three or even four times in the second and third years because it really is important to achieve the right shape, tapering very slightly towards the top. This ensures that any substantial fall of snow cannot lie too heavily on the somewhat fragile top and so break or bend the branches.

When the hedge is beginning to reach the desired height, pick a few places along its length where you can measure the height. You may find the best way is to make a special measuring pole. If you trim these places accurately then you can tailor the remainder of the hedge to fit in and so obtain a pleasant evenness. If you wish to wave or undulate your hedge, then you will have to allow certain portions to grow longer than others. The best time of year for trimming an established hedge is in the late summer. Aim always to cut back to within a few centimetres or less of the previous year's growth. Use good shears or electric clippers and for ease of clearing up, work above a long plastic sheet placed on the ground at the base of the hedge. You can then collect the trimmings all at once instead of having to rake or sweep them into piles.

DISEASE AND PEST CONTROL If the healthy trees and shrubs are planted in the right way, at the right time and in the right place, they should normally have years of healthy and productive life ahead of them. They will be able to shrug off most attacks of any diseases that come their way and will not succumb to the depredations of insects. Occasionally a freak of weather or circumstances may so weaken a plant that a disease or pest attack can then enter and cause severe damage, but it is impossible to guard against this.

An experienced gardener will quickly see from the appearance of the plants if there is something seriously wrong and will then examine, diagnose and treat accordingly. A few trees, the various types of flowering cherries are examples, tend to suffer from attacks of certain diseases and annual spraying will prevent this. Cherries are sometimes disfigured by the ugly blisters of peach leaf curl, a fungus disease that is controlled by a spray with Bordeaux mixture or dithane. Occasionally a rare or unexpected infestation of aphids or caterpillars may take place. This will probably not seriously damage a healthy tree but will certainly disfigure and perhaps weaken it, so a clearance spray is advisable.

As a general rule tree and shrub leaves that have holes or nibbled edges are an indication of beetle or bee attack which on most occasions is not of great significance. More important is the complete disappearance of a leaf, with only the petiole remaining. This indicates serious caterpillar infestation and the tree should be sprayed at once before damage goes too far. A systemic insecticide, one which is absorbed by the leaves and retains the poison to affect any insect or caterpillar which eats or chews the leaves even a few weeks later, is the sensible type to use here.

Silver leaf is one of the few important diseases that affects the flowering cherries, some willows, hawthorn, laburnum and others. It usually begins by fungus spores entering a wound, so if you consider pruning a cherry (usually quite unnecessary) make sure that the wound is cleaned and painted with Arbrex or a similar protective disinfectant. Silver leaf shows by the characteristic colour of the leaf and by a brown core in the affected shoots. Cut right back to healthy wood and clean and paint the wounds carefully.

Acid-loving plants such as rhododendrons and ericas sometimes show their unhappiness with an alkaline or limy soil by producing pale, yellowing leaves instead of the normal healthy green. This is a sign of chlorosis, a lack of iron. It can be prevented by incorporating acid peat into the soil and by spraying with a chelated iron compound to provide the necessary element.

There are many pests and insects that attack garden plants and it is not always easy to identify them or to tell them apart, but in general they will all succumb to a pesticide applied in the form of a liquid spray or a powder, either to the plant itself or to the soil at its base. Make sure that the spray or powder reaches every part of the plant that might be affected. Some pesticides are known as persistent or systemic because they are absorbed by the plant system and live in the sap for up to a month or so, which means that any pest eating any part of that plant will be killed. Others are contact killers only, or have a 'knock down' effect which merely incapacitates the pest for a period, so when using this type of insecticide it is always advisable to re-apply the spray or whatever after two or three days to make sure that the pest is cleared.

Always remember that pesticides are necessarily poisons. Store them and use them with care and responsibility. Never use them in a high wind. The best time of day is the still of the evening when the air is quiet, when the sun is sinking, when the bees and beneficial insects have left for their homes and when you, the gardener, are in the physical and psychological state of being ready to knock off your garden work and wash thoroughly and change your clothes.

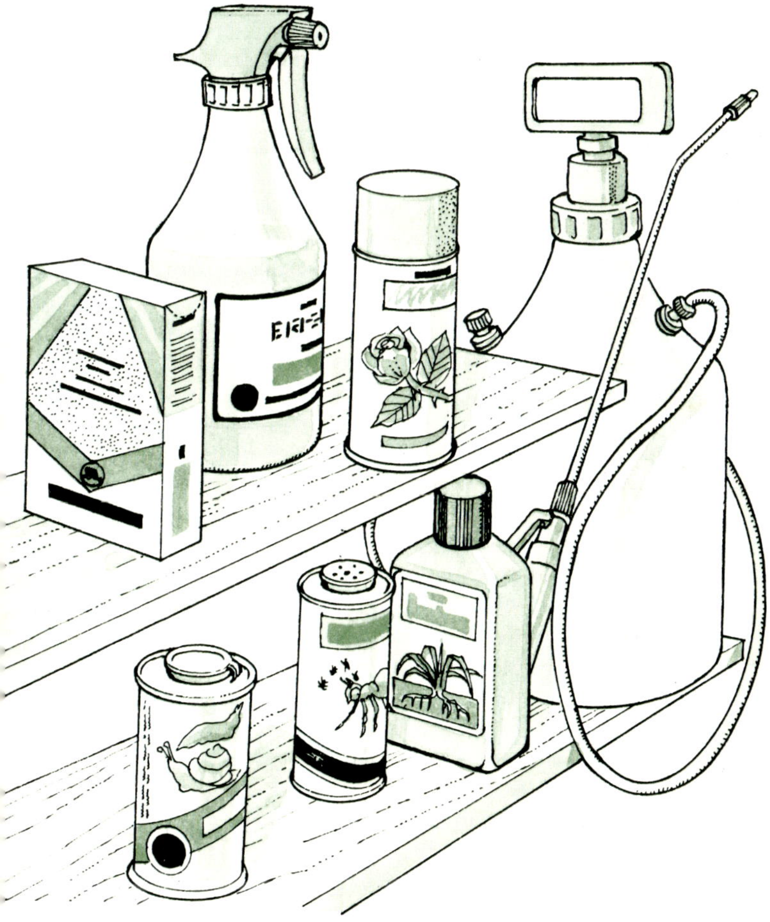

TRAINING AND PRUNING CALENDAR

Name	Mature Height in Metres	Value	Pruning
Abelia	1	fl	a
Acer	.5-20	fo	a
Amelanchier	6	fl, fo	a or b
Berberis	1-3	fl, ber	b, d
Calluna	.5-1	fl	d
Camellia	1.5	fl	c
Ceanothus	2	fl	c
Cercis	6	fl	a
Chaenomeles	2	fl, fr	a
Chamaecyparis	30	fo	a
Chimonanthus	3	fl	a
Corylopsis	3	fl	a
Cotoneaster (shrub)	2	fl, fo, ber	a
Cotoneaster (tree)	.5-5	fl, fo, ber	a
Crataegus	6	fl, ber	a
Cupressocyparis	25	fo	a
Cupressus	30	fo	a
Daphne	1	fl	a
Deutzia	2	fl	d
Elaeagnus	2	fo	a
Erica	.2-4	fl, fo	a
Escallonia	2-3	fl	a
Garrya	3	fr	a
Hamamelis	3	fl	a
Hebe	1.2	fl	b
Helianthemum	.2	fl	f, e
Juniperus	.5-5	fo	a
Kalmia	2	fl	f
Kolreuteria	10	fl	a
Mahonia	2	fl, ber	a
Malus	4	fl, fr	a
Morus	6	ber	a

Name	Mature Height in Metres	Value	Pruning
Olearia	2	fl	f
Osmanthus	2	fl	a
Pernettya	1	fl, ber	a
Philadelphus	3	fl	d
Pieris	3	fl, fo	a, f
Picea	20	fo	a
Potentilla	1	fl	a
Prunus (tree)	8	fl	a
Prunus (shrub)	5	fl, fo	a
Pyracantha	4	fl, ber	a, d
Pyrus	10	fl, fr	a
Rhus	4	fo	b
Ribes	2	fl	d
Salix	2-12	fo	a, b
Santolina	1	fl, fo	c, d
Senecio	1	fl, fo	a
Skimmia	1	fl, ber	a
Sorbus	2-10	fr	a
Spirea	3	fl	d, e
Taxus	.5-5	fo	a
Viburnum	3	fl	a
Weigela	2	fl	d

fl – flowers; fo – foliage; fr – fruit; ber – berries.

a No regular pruning. Cut out damaged or diseased branches and prune to size in February.

b Cut back in February.

c Cut back in April.

d Shorten flowering branches after flowering.

e Cut flowering branches almost to base after flowering.

f Dead head.

PLANT STOCK

WHAT TO LOOK FOR WHEN BUYING PLANTS

Young trees and shrubs suitable for growing in the garden are available from a number of sources. Some types of plants are sold in supermarkets and a somewhat wider range is available from the high street garden shop. The garden centre presents a whole range of plants, nearly always in containers ready for immediate planting. The nursery has its plants growing in the soil and it is necessary to give the staff there some notice so that the trees or shrubs can be dug from the soil and the roots wrapped for transportation. Finally, there are a number of mail order organizations, some selling by means of advertisements in newspapers or gardening journals, others reaching customers by catalogue.

There is no best place to buy; all depends on the skill, experience, honesty and facilities offered by the retailer. Perhaps it is helpful, however, to point out one or two danger signs. The supermarket and to some extent the high street shop usually sell their shrubs as pre-packed specimens for obvious reasons. It is not easy to tell how long these specimens have been out of the soil or how dry they have become. So ask for this information and examine as carefully as you can. Container-grown plants in most garden centres are to be trusted, for apart from anything else you can examine them easily and reject any samples that have falling or drooping leaves, protruding roots, weak or broken stems, or signs of insect attack. Give the plant a light tug and if it comes easily out of the container look at the roots. They are almost certainly sparse and weak, indicating that the shrub has not been growing in the container but has only recently been placed there, so do not buy it. But on the other hand, if the roots are visible above the soil surface, thick and strong, then this indicates that the plant has been too long in the container and will not adapt easily to planting in the open ground.

It is not always easy to examine thoroughly a pre-packaged plant such as might be sold in a supermarket or similar establishment, but if the packages look weary and handled and if the temperature of the store is high, then the plants would have little chance of flourishing and they should be rejected. It might be possible to see one or two weak or dried-out stems, which of course would be an indication of poor health. If buying from an advertisement in a newspaper or gardening journal, do not be carried away by the high-flown prose. If the plants offered were as strong, as beautiful, as easily grown, as quick to flourish and mature as the advertisement claims, then ask yourself why they are being offered at such a comparatively low price. This type of plant is often given a popular name of great appeal, but if you can look up the correct botanical name you are likely to find that it is not as romantic, as beautiful nor indeed as suitable as it is claimed to be in the advertisement.

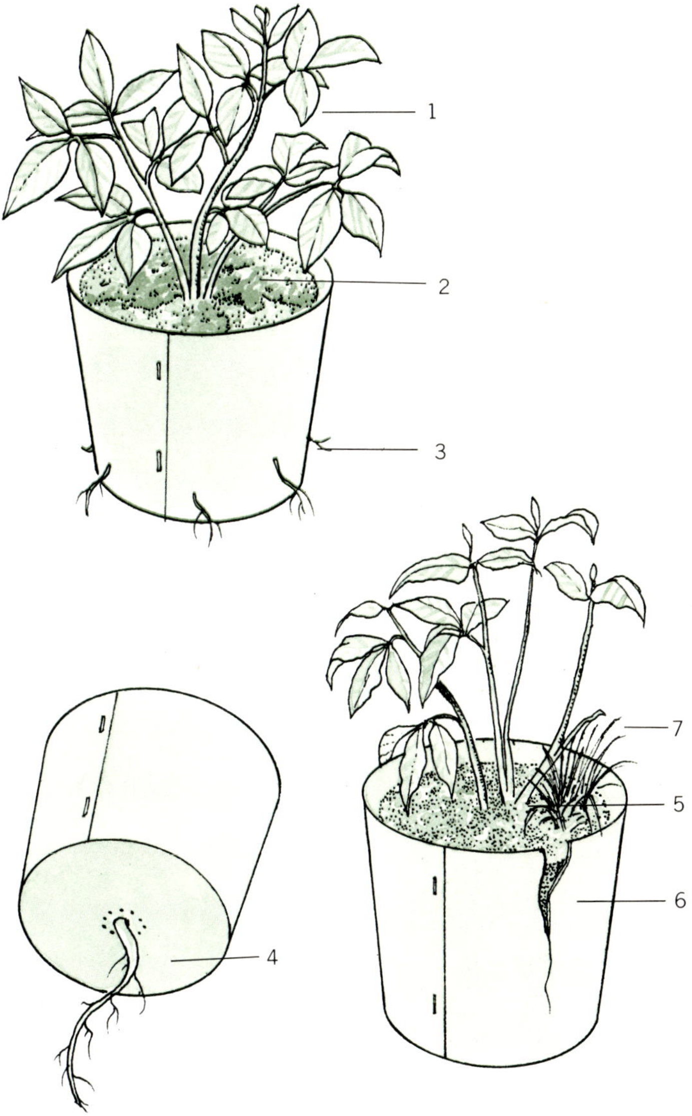

Good signs in container-grown plants include firmly bedded plants (1); a few weeds or green algae on the soil (2); small roots coming through the container (3). A thick root growing from the base is a bad sign showing that the plant has been in the container too long or is starving (4); as do thick, exposed roots on the surface (5). A split container denotes an old plant (6); and dense weed growth shows that the soil is no good (7).

1

2

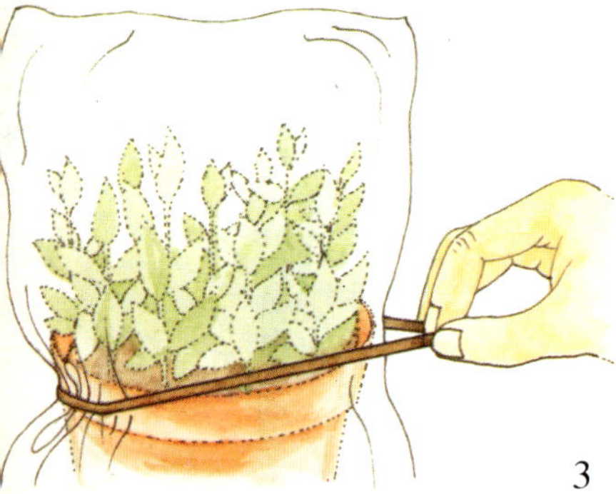

3

4

RAISING PLANTS FROM SEED AND CUTTINGS

By far the cheapest way of raising trees and shrubs is to grow them from seed and the fact that this is done so seldom indicates that there must be some good reason. Seed of some plants is difficult to obtain and most are difficult to germinate without special conditions of heat and humidity. Those shrubs which can be raised easily enough from seed include leycesteria, genista, cistus and potentilla and the problem when raising these will be that of disposing of the many plants produced.

Fill a pot in spring with seed compost and water it, then sprinkle the seed very gently on the surface and cover with the lightest sprinkling of sand. Slip a plastic bag over the pot and secure it in place with a rubber band, placing the pot in a warm but shaded position. When the seeds have begun to germinate, move the pot to a spot where there is plenty of light but no direct sun and open the plastic bag to allow air to enter. When the seedlings can be handled move them, one to each small pot filled with a good potting compost, and then when the little plants have achieved a safe size put them in the garden.

The easiest way to raise new trees and shrubs is by taking cuttings, either in winter outdoors or in summer in the greenhouse. Take hardwood cuttings in

October or November, choosing shoots of mature wood up to 30cm (12in) long. With deciduous plants the leaves will have fallen, with evergreens strip the low half of all foliage. Make a shallow trench some 15-20cm (6-8in) deep in a sheltered part of the garden, one side upright, the other sloping. Drop 5cm (2in) or so of sharp sand into the base of this trench. Now dip the lowest end of the cutting into some hormone rooting powder (5) and then stand it in the trench against the vertical wall so that the base rests on the layer of sand. Fill in the trench and firm down the soil. Roots will begin to grow when the days get longer and warmer in the spring and by autumn new growth will be evident.

While they are passing their winter in the soil, visit the site occasionally to make sure the cuttings have not been smothered by falling leaves or otherwise damaged. If there has been heavy frost it is possible that the soil has been raised a little, in which case press it down again.

In summer take half-ripe cuttings, choosing a stem about 15cm (6in) long, soft and green at the tip and becoming woody at the base. Strip the leaves from the lower half (1), dip into rooting hormone (see below) and then insert in a pot filled with potting compost (2). After watering gently, cover the pot with a plastic bag and seal (3). Keep in a lightly shaded cool place until growth is visible in spring (4).

5

LAYERING AND DIVISION Two further means of increasing your stock of trees and shrubs are the processes of layering and division, both even easier than taking cuttings because the shrub does all the work for you!

For layering it is necessary to have a plant which is low growing or has flexible branches low down near the soil. In spring or autumn take one of these branches and bend it down until it touches the soil. Where it touches, gently cut half through the wood and slip a matchstick or something similar into the gash to hold it just open. Bury this portion of the stem in the soil, pegging it down just 5cm (2in) or so beneath the surface with a twig or perhaps even a hairpin. Prop up the green and growing tip on a stone or tie it to a small stake or twig. In anything from six to twelve months you will see from the increased activity at this stem end that new roots have been made. They will be at the point where you made a nick in the stem. Cut away the old stem portion between these roots and the parent plant. Leave the new young plant to make stronger roots for a few more months and then transfer it to its permanent home in the garden. Suitable plants for this type of layering include forsythia, honeysuckle, rhododendrons (above right), lilac, camellias and ericas.

An even easier form of propagation is known as division and it consists of dividing or separating some of the spreading growth of an existing tree or shrub which normally grows in clumps. Examples are kerria, rhus, ceratostigma, stephanandra, pachysandra, romneya and *Cornus alba* (below right).

Examine your plant carefully and see where a portion is obviously growing apart from the main or parent plant. Thrust your spade strongly into the ground all around this smaller, separate plant to cut the roots which join it to the parent. Then dig it up with as much root as possible, transport it to its new site and replant, watering in well and keeping the soil moist for the first few weeks.

Sometimes it may be easier to dig up the whole of the parent plant and then cut away one or more portions to be planted separately. So long as no part of the plant is out of the soil more than a few minutes, no harm should come to either parent plant or the divided portion, but again keep the soil moist in time of drought. The best time to choose is late autumn for deciduous plants and spring or autumn for evergreens.

Still another means of propagating plants from your own or a neighbour's garden is that of grafting. This is a much more complex technique involving a certain dexterity and skill that comes only from experience or sound tuition. No useful purpose would be served in giving sketchy details here. The previous methods described on these pages are relatively simple and almost foolproof. Grafting is a technique best left to the professionals.

Layering a rhododendron

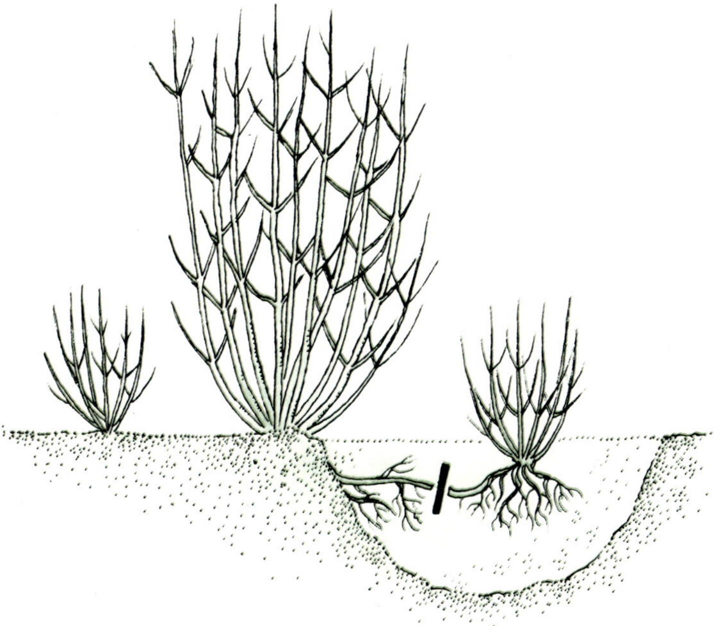

Dividing a cornus

SPECIAL QUALITIES

COLOURED AND VARIEGATED PLANTS

Some of the glories of our gardens are provided not by the brilliant colours of the flowers but by the more muted hues of trees and shrubs, for not only are the leaves in several tints and hues of green, but they also come in white, cream, yellow, gold, orange, red, purple, silver, grey and glaucous blue-green. Some of these colours are encompassed in the normal life cycle of the tree or shrub, beginning in the spring with the soft green breaking of the opening buds, the colour gradually losing its yellow and turning a darker green until autumn when the chlorophyll disappears and the leaves turn brown and fall or perhaps become a more spectacular orange and yellow and scarlet before they go.

Many varieties of trees and shrubs maintain a striking leaf colour during the season, and some evergreens hold their colour throughout their lives. These permanent plants with variegated foliage are of the greater value for they enable us to create permanent blocks of colour of particular importance in the winter, when among the dark and dismal leaflessness suddenly shines through the cheerful gold of *Chamaecyparis lawsoniana* 'Lanei Aurea' or one of the other invaluable golden evergreens.

It is impossible to draw a firm and definite line between the various coloured foliages but in their rough categories here are a few of the best of these fine plants. Among those trees with variegated white, cream or pale yellow leaves perhaps the most spectacular and beautiful is the poplar, *Populus candicans* 'Aurora', which produces white, cream, green and pink leaves in the late spring. These fantastic colours do not last, but they are wonderful when they are there. Look also for some of the variegated maples and the lovely gold-edged leaves of the tulip tree, *Liriodendron tulipifera* 'Aureo marginatum'.

There are too many cream and gold variegated shrubs to mention, many of them evergreen, from *Abelia chinensis* 'Frances Mason' through to the variegated forms of the spiky yucca, but look particularly for some of the hollies and phormiums, the euonymus and the elaeagnus. There are even several silver and golden variegated climbers.

Some of the most useful trees and shrubs are in the gold spectrum. Among trees the golden beech and the golden poplar are recommended and the beautiful *Robinia pseudoacacia* 'Frisia' has leaves which are wonderfully coloured and attractively shaped. Among shrubs seek out *Catalpa bignonioides* 'Aurea', *Acer japonicum* 'Aureum' and the golden privet, elder and flowering currant.

Acer palmatum

HABIT AND RATE OF GROWTH

Horticultural nomenclature is generally fairly intelligible once explained, but some words have a slightly different meaning from that in general use. The 'habit' of a plant, for example, means the overall appearance in relation to its manner of growth. So a tree is said to be erect or weeping, bushy or prostrate. This, then, is its natural habit of growth.

'Growth' is dependent to some extent on the habit. An erect tree, for example, will tend to grow upwards rather than outwards. So growth can be defined as the increase in size by cell division and expansion, made permanent by the thickening of cell walls and the formation of supporting and strengthening tissues such as fibre and wood — all of which may sound technical but is necessary to help explain some of the elementary essentials of modern gardening.

It is important to take note of these recorded characteristics. We read, for example, that a conifer is of prostrate habit and moderate growth. This could indicate that it will be suitable to

1. Columnar or fastigiate

2. Pyramidal or conical

cover and conceal an unattractive drainage inspection cover. Or it could prevent the frequently committed sin of planting a tender and beautiful young weeping willow in the vacant space in front of a living room window. Although the young tree will present an enchanting picture for the first two or three years, it will increasingly fill all the available space and darken the room and will eventually be taken down, only to leave a large and disfiguring stump to be concealed.

This same tree planted further down the garden could serve first to disguise and then conceal the factory chimney, for example, or to create a natural playground for the children.

With some plants and under certain circumstances it is possible to alter its habit in order to make it more useful or even more attractive, but as a general rule this is both unwise and counter-productive. When an erect growing plant is used with other similar plants to make a hedge or barrier, it is possible to stem the upright habit of growth by clipping or cutting away the top. This stimulates side growth and is normally successful, so that instead of having a plant with erect habit, you have one with a more suitable spreading nature.

All good lists and catalogues of plants give an indication of their habit and growth. Growth, for example, is usually quoted as an average height and spread for a mature tree or shrub. Maturity is usually reached in about 10 to 15 years. It is therefore a comparatively simple matter to decide whether or not a tree or shrub is likely to fit the space available for the foreseeable future.

3. Weeping or pendulous

4. Globular or round

SCENTED FLOWERS AND AROMATIC FOLIAGE

There is a tendency to dismiss all trees and many shrubs as a source of garden perfumes, expecting scent only from the flowers of herbaceous materials and a few shrubs such as roses, lavender and witch hazel. Yet many plants are perfumed.

The leaves of eucalyptus trees are of course scented, as are the leaves of *Populus balsamifera* with their perfume of balsam, but the boundaries of smell extend much further. Many leaves are used in various aspects of scents, unguents, salves and in cookery. Leaves of *Laurus nobilis*, the bay tree, have been used in the kitchen for years, as have those of the sage, *Salvia officinalis*, and of rosemary. Lavender leaves and flowers are well known particularly in pot pourri and body perfumes. Some varieties of cistus produce a sap or gum so fragrant that it is used in the manufacture of perfumes.

It is the flowers that really provide the perfumes, as would be expected, although it is not generally realized just how many flowering trees are scented. The blooms of the flowering crabs and cherries are rich in scent. One of the mountain ashes, *Sorbus esserteauana*, gives strongly scented flowers in late spring, while the manna or flowering ash, *Fraxinus ornus*, produces perfumed white blooms just before this. Several of the tilias or limes are so strongly perfumed that the air is

Philadelphus

Lavandula spica

scented all around them and attracts the bees in the neighbourhood to their creamy yellow flowers in June or July.

Shrubs provide us with the widest possible list of perfumed flowers and how grateful we are for some of the earliest to scent the air in spring. In the darkest days of winter, scent is provided by the flowers of *Viburnum farreri* (also known as *V. fragrans*), of wintersweet, *Chimonanthus praecox*, and the witch hazel, *Hamamelis mollis* and *H. pallida*. For the remainder of the year there is a constant flow of perfume from flowering shrubs such as the mahonias, elaeagnus, lavenders, syringas, buddleias, daphnes and many more. How surprising, for example, to discover the powerful scent of vanilla emanating from the miniature yellow flowers of *Azara microphylla* and to identify the well-known Spanish broom, *Spartium junceum*, as the source of a honey smell.

Among the climbers to provide familiar scents are jasmine and honeysuckle, myrtle and mimosa.

Most gardeners could make better use of their garden perfumes. Instead of spreading them about and so lessening their impact, they could concentrate them where they would be enjoyed to greatest advantage. Plant honeysuckle and species roses to waft their scents into the open bedroom windows in summer.

ORNAMENTAL FRUITS, BARK AND WOOD

We tend to favour various trees and shrubs because of their striking foliage or their beautiful flowers, thinking too seldom of the other advantages they may possess. Fruits and berries, both of which are merely seed capsules, can be beautiful too, as can bark colour. How fascinating are the peeling and curling barks of *Betula papyrifera* and *Acer griseum*, and the brilliant red of *Cornus alba* 'Sibirica'. No garden is complete without some examples of the variety of nature as expressed not merely in flowers and foliage but in other ways.

If you are fortunate enough to have the space to grow one, look at the flowers of a horse chestnut tree, like a pyramid of tiny orchids, each flower exquisitely formed and coloured. These will be followed by large, rounded, prickly fruits containing the glossy conkers so beloved of small children. There are luscious round or conical fruits on crab trees, golden or scarlet, cherry-like or almost as large as eating apples. There are long, twisted pods on a honey locust, *Gleditschia triacanthos*, and the extraordinary bladder-like fruits of *Koelreuteria paniculata*. Medlars from the mespilus and mulberries from the *Morus nigra* can be collected and enjoyed. If birds allow you, you can have colourful berries — white, yellow, pink, orange or red — on sorbus trees.

Perhaps not quite so dramatic, the range of fruits presented

Cornus alba 'Sibirica'

Arbutus unedo 'Rubra'

by the shrubs in our gardens can be even wider than those found on trees. Every colour is represented, ranging from amelanchier, with its shining red summer fruits deepening to almost black, to vitis, many of which have edible grapes.

The strawberry tree, arbutus, gives exceptional value with cinnamon-coloured bark, lily-of-the-valley flowers and the simultaneous large strawberry-like fruits. *Symphoricarpus albus*, the snowberry, produces white or pink berries and grows strongly. The quinces provc profitable with useful fruits following their vivid flowers. If you have bushes of both sexes, the hippophae will produce an abundance of semi-translucent orange berries. For a change grow *Corylus maxima* 'Purpurea' and get purple hazel nuts, not the normal brown, as richly coloured as the abundant foliage.

You can expect berries on viburnums, hollies, berberis, cotoneaster, pyracantha and skimmia. Less well-known shrubs which can provide a fruitful autumn include *Callicarpa bodinieri*, with violet berries; *Dorycnium hirsutum*, bearing fruit pods tinged with red; *Osmanthus decora*, purple-black berries; *Colutea arborescens*, with swollen pods like bladders; *Gaultheria procumbens*, bright red berries; *Ruscus aculeatus*, with curious leaves which bear scarlet berries in their centres; and *Rhamnus frangula*, with fruits beginning as red and changing gradually to a deep black.

SMALL TREES

ACER There are something like 150 deciduous species of acers known mainly as maples, sometimes as sycamores, most of them easy to grow and highly decorative. Trees and shrubs are grown predominantly for their timber, the form and colour of their foliage and for the interesting bark produced by some species. The flowers are small, insignificant, clustered and greenish yellow. The fruits consist of two wings like a propeller, joined at the centre by the two seeds. *A. campestre*, the common or field maple, can be grown as a hedge but will also reach more than 20m (65ft) in height. There are also *A. platanoides*, the Norway maple; *A. pseudoplatanus*, the common sycamore; acers for leaf colour, for beautiful bark and perhaps best of all, the Japanese maples, *A. palmatum*, with five- or seven-lobed leaves. Maples like a moist, well-drained soil and some protection from strong winds.

AMELANCHIER A deciduous tree or shrub known as snowy mespilus or June berry, it will grow to 5m (16ft) or more

Amelanchier canadensis

and will make a spreading and bushy shrub. Of the dozen or so species and varieties available, the best for most gardens is probably *A. lamarckii*, which has silky, copper-red leaves becoming more vivid in the autumn. Starry white flowers are produced in spring, hanging in long racemes and developing into crimson fruits which gradually turn black and shining. Several species are often wrongly named as *A. canadensis*, the service berry, which has downy leaves when young and little edible berries. Another good species is *A. laevis*, particularly beautiful in spring, when the profusion of starry white flowers shows well against the somewhat sparse pink leaves.

CERCIS The only member of this deciduous pea family tree or shrub that appears to be well known is the familiar Judas tree, *C. siliquastrum*, so called because of the legend that Judas hanged himself on it. This is a pity, for several of the half dozen or so species available to us are worth growing in our gardens so long as the site is not too cold and windy, for cercis trees like full sun and good drainage at their roots. The Judas tree has clusters of pink to purple pea-like flowers in spring on bare branches. The variety 'Alba' has white flowers. *C. canadensis*, the North American red bud, also has pale, almost white flowers. Some species are somewhat slow to flower, spending their first years preparing themselves for the event.

Cercis siliquastrum

COTONEASTER This is a splendid plant which will grow in any soil, in sun or shade, evergreen and deciduous, as a prostrate ground hugger or as a tree up to 6m (19ft) tall. It produces masses of pretty little pinkish-white flowers in spring that are loved by the bees and follows these flowers with berries, mainly red or orange. It has leaves that can be tiny or comparatively large and none of the hundred or more species and varieties has any spines or thorns to tear fingers or clothes. Perhaps the most popular and most used cotoneaster is *C. horizontalis*, growing in flat, fan-like branches with the stems arching out like a fishbone, thick with flowers in spring, covered with berries in autumn. This is one of the convenient plants that can be used as a ground cover to hide a manhole cover, yet it will also lean decoratively and protectively against a wall or fence. It is not evergreen, but several species which are include *C. conspicuus* 'Decorus' and *C. salicifolius* 'Autumn Fire', both with scarlet berries.

CRATAEGUS Like the cotoneaster, crataegus is a member of the rose family. Known popularly as hawthorn or may, these are the last of the spring-flowering trees, decorating the countryside with their masses of white flowers in late May or early June and following these in autumn with the haws —

Cotoneaster horizontalis

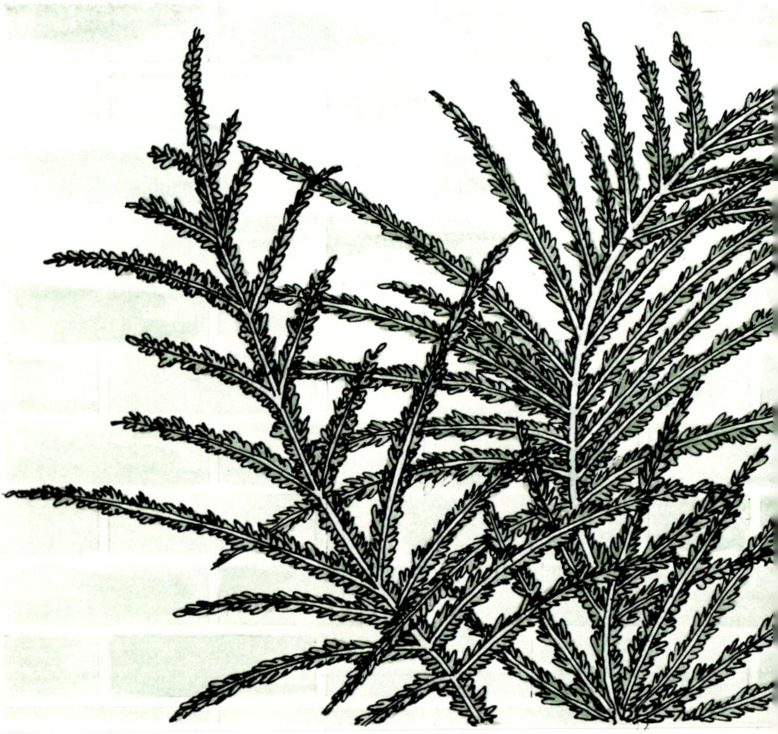

their shining berries, usually red, sometimes orange. Once they are established, hawthorns will grow under almost any conditions, in the industrial smoke and at the salt-laden seaside. The best known species is *C. monogyna*, the common may, hawthorn or quick, so called because of its convenient ability to grow and take root quickly after the most casual thrusting of a twig into the soil. It has perfumed white flowers and powerful thorns, which are a considerable assistance in its function as a hedge. There are, however, species which are almost thornless.

KOELREUTERIA An interesting and attractive genus normally represented in our gardens by only one species. It makes a tree which will grow to 5m (16ft), bearing pinnate leaves made up of ten or so oval leaflets which begin as red in spring, turn a pale yellow, then green and finally become bright yellow in autumn. The leaves are probably one reason for one of its popular names, golden rain tree. The yellow flowers appear in mid-summer and are followed by curious brown-bronze bladders bearing the seeds. Best-known species is *K. paniculata*, which develops into a mop-headed medium-sized tree. A variety, *apiculata*, rarely seen, differs only in having more leaves.

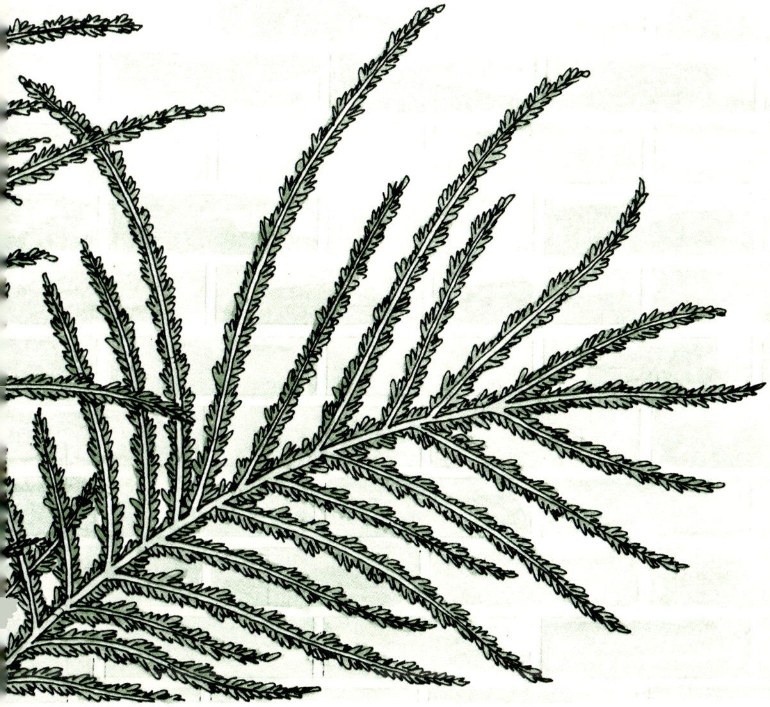

MALUS The malus or flowering crab is said to provide more examples of small trees for the garden than any other genus with the possible exception of prunus, the flowering cherries. Certainly the crabs are highly decorative with their masses of white, pink or red flowers in April or May to be followed by the ornamental and sometimes edible fruits in the autumn. Malus and prunus can be differentiated by a glance at the flowers, for the malus has five styles in the centre and prunus only one. With the fruits, malus has a series of apple-like pips in the centre while prunus has only the one almond-like stone. Best-known favourite is probably 'John Downie', with white flowers followed by large crab apples, brilliantly coloured with orange and yellow. 'Golden Hornet' has rich yellow rounder fruits. A fairly modern hybrid, 'Profusion', brings masses of fragrant, wine-red flowers, with copper-red foliage and very dark red fruits, and *M. tschonoskii* is upright, conical, with pinky-white flowers, yellow fruits and vivid leaves of yellow, orange, scarlet and almost purple in the autumn.

MORUS Sadly neglected, the mulberry is not always easy to find in nurseries or garden centres. The tree is comparatively small and slow growing, yet well clothed with attractive leaves. It outlives most of us and produces an abundance of fruits that are quite unique in flavour and texture. It is said that trees are slow to fruit until they reach a considerable age, but this is not so with modern cultivars, which will fruit abundantly when only four or five years old. Look for *Morus nigra*, the black mulberry, rather than *M. alba*, the white, for the latter is the one on which the silkworms feed, not the fruiting species.

PRUNUS The family is a wide one, including all the Japanese cherries, the almond, apricot, peach, bird cherry and both common and Portugal laurels. They grow well in almost any soil, generally preferring lime, enjoy full sun and produce flowers with prodigality. There are forms that grow spire-like upwards and those that are drooping and pendulous. There are species like *P. subhirtella autumnalis* that will be in flower almost every day from November to April or later, right through the winter. There are species with purple leaves, among which is the well-known *P. cerasifera* 'Pissardii', grown frequently as an attractive and highly efficient hedging plant. There are many Japanese flowering cherries, most of them bearing Japanese names like the favourite 'Amanogawa', the columnar pillar of spring blossom which is such a space saver in a small garden. Some of the foliage is a beautiful bronze, especially when young. Some flowers are double, some single. Ornamental plum, peach, almond and cherry are apt to suffer from peach leaf curl, a fungus disease, so a preventive spray early in the year is advisable.

Malus floribunda

Pyrus salicifolia 'Pendula'

PYRUS This is another small, decorative tree from the productive rose family. The decorative pear will grow in almost any soil, in sun or shade, in moist or dry, in cold or heat. It is tolerant of atmospheric pollution and demands no special attention, no special pruning. There are fewer pyrus species than prunus and malus, but sheer quality has forced *P. salicifolia* to the foreground and it is now to be seen everywhere. This is the willow-leaved pear, with attractive leaves covered in spring with a silvery fuzz which later turns a whitish green. There are white flowers in spring. The common form is the pendulous one, with branches sweeping downwards from the domed crown of the tree. A specimen that grows upwards rather than down is *P. calleryana*, with green leaves which turn red in winter. The species *nivalis* has a foam of white flowers against a background of silvery white foliage.

SALIX The willows are agreeable trees that fulfil a number of garden tasks in a quiet and modest manner. They are perhaps best appreciated for their appearance in weeping form and *S. chrysocoma*, the golden weeping willow, can be one of our most beautiful trees though it should have plenty of space around it, preferably with water nearby, for it to look its best. Unfortunately too often it is placed where it will quickly crowd the space allotted to it and subsequent frantic pruning and lopping will ruin its appearance. In these situations it is far better to choose the smaller growing *Salix purpurea* 'Pendula', the American weeping willow. There are a number of non-weeping willows, all of them interesting, easy and fast growing, a useful attribute with a new garden and convenient because none of the willows resents a certain amount of pruning and cutting about. Try the fast-growing cricket bat willow, *S.* 'Caerulea', oval in shape with purple shoots or *S. daphnoides*, the violet willow.

SORBUS Another invaluable member of the Rosaceae, the rose family, the sorbus is neatly divided into the aucuparias or mountain ashes and the arias or whitebeams, all of which grow well under most conditions, are hardy, tolerant of pollution and even of seaside salt sprays. *S. aucuparia*, the mountain ash or rowan, is familiar enough and has a number of varieties, all of which produce clusters of red or orange fruits or berries in autumn, quickly devoured by the birds. *S. aria* is said to be one of the best trees for coastal, windswept and industrial areas and is particularly at home on a chalky soil. The leaves are simple as opposed to pinnate in the aucuparias. The whitebeams have a foliage which is greyish-white at first, later turning green, then gold and red when the scarlet fruits appear.

Salix daphnoides

CONIFERS

CHAMAECYPARIS The so-called false cypress, chamaecyparis, covers those species of conifers with flat branches and small cones. It is known mainly for the Lawson cypress, *C. lawsoniana*, with its long list of invaluable varieties, some dwarf, some tall, some quick growing and some slow. Most dislike strong winds and hence exposed sites and enjoy a moist but well-drained soil. *C. lawsoniana* 'Elwoodii' is a slow growing, upright tree with dark green foliage which turns almost glaucous in winter. It will grow to about 2m (6ft), as will the attractive *C.l.* 'Minima Aurea', which makes a dense cone of soft, golden-yellow foliage. Because they are slow to grow, this does not mean that they will not become large in time, so make sure before you plant. Other chamaecyparis species include *obtusa* and its varieties, usually but not always growing to larger trees, conical in shape.

CUPRESSOCYPARIS This family, derived from a cross between the cupressus and the chamaecyparis, is known mainly for the important and useful *C. leylandii*, a large tree but nevertheless used frequently for tall hedges simply because of its extremely rapid rate of growth. It is said to be the fastest growing conifer, putting on more than 1m (3ft) a year. The varieties usually grown are those with a fastigiate or narrowly columnar habit of growth. This is an easy species to grow.

CUPRESSUS This branch of the conifer family is generally rather more tricky to grow. They are apt to suffer in cold winters and can be difficult to transplant and care for when very young. It is best always to buy pot-grown plants and when planting them to make sure that the root ball is undamaged. Most soils are tolerated except those that are very wet, but strong or salt-laden winds can damage young plants. *C. macrocarpa*, the Monterey cypress, may still be seen in some gardens but because it loses its lower branches easily and suffers from cold, it is grown less often than in the past. Travellers who have seen so many cypress trees in the Mediterranean regions will often try the Italian or Mediterranean cypress, *C. sempervirens*, a medium-sized tree with a narrowly columnar habit and dark green foliage. It is subject to some damage in colder districts but if planted sensibly will prove an asset to the garden. There are two varieties, 'Gracilis', even slimmer than the type, raised in New Zealand, and 'Swaines Gold', a more compact form.

Cupressus arizonica 'Bonita'

JUNIPERUS This is a large genus of useful garden conifers ranging from prostrate plants to thick shrubs and tall, columnar and conical trees, all of which have aromatic foliage and grey-green berries. *J. virginiana* 'Skyrocket' is said to be the slimmest of all columnar conifers. It grows to about 3m (10ft). It is in the rock garden and the erica bed that junipers fit most neatly, for some of the low and slow-growing specimens complement the other small shrubs around them; colours blend as well as the textures. The common juniper, *J. communis*, presents a number of interesting and useful varieties, of which *J.c.* 'Compressa', dwarf, compact and slow growing, is one of the best. Another is *J.c.* 'Depressa', the Canadian juniper, spreading and ground hugging, with brownish-red foliage in winter. There is a golden form, 'Depressa aurea'. The *Juniperus macrocarpa* 'Pfitzeriana' is said to be one of the most commonly planted of all conifers. It is spreading, making a good ground cover, yet grows sufficiently tall for it to make a good specimen for the lawn or to be used as a focal point in a border. 'The Pfitzer Juniper is a friend of the landscape gardener', says Hillier's famous manual. 'It never lets him down, it marries the formal into the informal, it embellishes his layout and hides his errors.' What a tribute!

PICEA The spruces present a wider range of sizes and shapes in various tones of green, a little more choosy and temperamental when it comes to planting soils and conditions than some of the other conifers. The first to be mentioned should, of course, be perhaps the most famous tree in the western world, the Christmas tree, *Picea abies*, not one of the best trees for the garden. The dwarf variety, *P.a.* 'Pygmea', is compact and globular, said to grow at a rate of less than 1cm (½in) a year. 'Brewer's Weeping Spruce', *P. breweriana*, makes a small to medium conical tree with spreading branches from which droop and hang a veritable curtain of smaller blue-green branchlets.

TAXUS The yews, a comparatively small genus, appear to be confined to ancient churchyards, where they have certainly proved their worth. They are excellent slow-growing trees and shrubs, unusually tolerant of shade and able to grow well in almost any soil. One reason for the neglect of this useful tree is that the bright red berries are said to be poisonous to humans. It is not the berries or the fleshy part that is poisonous but the seed, which humans naturally enough do not eat. The foliage will poison cattle, particularly when it is dry or withered. *T. baccata*, the common yew, is said to live for more than 1000 years. *T.b.* 'Fastigiata', the Irish yew, is upright, columnar, highly architectural and *T.b.* 'Fastigiata aureo marginata' is even more beautiful with its yellow-edged foliage.

Picea pungens

EVERGREEN SHRUBS

ABELIA Graceful, generous and decorative flowering shrubs, these can hold their white to pink flowers from June to October. Some varieties are semi-evergreen, others deciduous, and a severe winter can kill a plant, so wherever possible site abelia in the protection of a wall or among other shrubs so that it gains in warmth and shelter but still gets the benefit of full sun. The best of the semi-evergreen varieties include 'Edward Goucher' with a multitude of lilac-pink flowers; *A. floribunda*, producing abundant vivid red tubular flowers in June; and *A. grandiflora*, bearing pink and white blooms from June to September. The soil for abelias should be moist but well drained and the site in full sun.

BERBERIS Of the many barberries available, all are spiny and so make good hedging material. They nearly all have yellow flowers; some are so small as to be beautiful in the rock garden while others make huge bushes; some are deciduous and some evergreen. *B. darwinii*, evergreen and early flowering, is one of the best of all flowering shrubs, with dark glossy green leaves and long bunches of yellow flowers, crimson tinted, in April and May followed by the round, purple berries in autumn. There are a dozen or so varieties of a favourite, *B. stenophylla*, evergreen and graceful, with long arching stems covered in yellow flowers in April. *B. insignis* is particularly valuable with its long, smooth, yellow stems carrying clusters of leaves, green above and yellow beneath.

CALLUNA This is a genus with only a single species, a lime-hater that can only be grown successfully in an acid soil, often grouped collectively with erica, from which it differs by its four-parted corolla and calyx. But although only one species exists, there are several score of varieties, with both flowers and foliage of various colours all blooming in late summer, yet as evergreens providing interest the year through. One of the best of these heathers is 'Robert Chapman' because its foliage begins in spring as gold, changes to orange and finally to red, while the purple flowers appear in late summer. 'H.E. Beale', perhaps the best known of the callunas, produces its long racemes of soft pink double flowers rather later, between September and November. 'Joy Vanstone' has orchid-pink flowers and a lovely gold foliage which deepens to orange in winter. The famed Scottish heather, so visible over the moors, is *C. vulgaris* and there is a double version, *C.v.* 'Alba plena'.

Berberis lologensis
Calluna vulgaris

Camellia williamsii

CAMELLIA This is one of the best of all evergreen shrubs, with crisp, shining green foliage and magnificent flowers between March and May. Camellias have the reputation of being difficult and tender, yet if grown in an acid soil and given some protection from cold winds and frosts, plants will do well and amply repay what little attention they demand. They grow well in tubs and other containers. There are hundreds of varieties, most of them from *C. japonica*, and it is usual to make a choice by the colours and sizes of the blooms. Some varieties are definitely only for mild districts, but many others will grow in most areas and climates with only a little sensible protection. Some of the best camellias to grow are the Williamsii, exceptionally free flowering over a period from November to May. Naturally enough, 'J.C. Williams' is a first choice, a medium single with phlox-pink flowers. 'Donation', orchid pink, large and semi-double, is also popular. Another is 'Citation', a silvery blush pink, large, semi-double and there is a splendid single white named 'Francis Hanger'. The earliest of the group to flower, in November, is the medium single, phlox-pink 'November Pink'.

COTONEASTER This invaluable shrub is another member of the rose family and can be grown almost anywhere, on any soil, in sun or shade. Cotoneasters can be deciduous or evergreen, can have tiny leaves or large. Practically without exception the white flowers so loved by bees open about June and are followed later in the year by profuse numbers of orange, red or yellow berries. There are no thorns on any varieties. Cotoneasters can roughly be divided into three types:

those that are prostrate and cover the ground, those that are of medium growth some 30cm (12in) to 1m (3ft) tall and those that are even taller, making small trees. Of the prostrate type, *C. dammeri*, *C. hybridus pendulus* and *C. salicifolius pendulus* all have red berries, while *C.* 'Skogholm Coral Beauty', as the name suggests, has berries of a vivid orange. All are evergreen. Best of the tall cotoneasters is *C. lacteus*.

ELAEAGNUS A useful shrub, this is grown generally for its foliage rather than its abundance of small, scented silvery-white flowers. The shrub grows quickly and is highly wind resistant, so it is natural that it is much used for hedging, where it even withstands the strong, salt-laden winds near the sea. One of the best evergreen species is *E. ebbingei*, which has large leaves, silver underneath, and white flowers in the autumn followed by orange fruits in spring. Particularly striking is *E. pungens* 'Maculata'.

Elaeagnus pungens 'Dicksonii'

ERICA The ericas, like the callunas, lings and daboecias, appear to be grouped together under the common name of heather or heath and as long as the correct botanical label can be pinned onto the correct plants there seems to be no reason why this should not be so. The ericas, with the exception of a few species mentioned below, are all lime-haters, all comparatively easy to grow, all like sun rather than shade, all spread and develop well. They range from dwarf, prostrate plants to the tree heaths that can grow to 5m (16ft) and the range of colours, both in flower and in foliage, is now so wide that it is possible to have plants in decorative condition for nearly 12 months in the year. The tree heath is *E. arborea* and there is a hardier, more upright form, *E.a.* 'Alpina'. The major species of ericas that will grow in an alkaline soil are *E. carnea*, *E. darleyensis* and *E. mediterranea*. All have a considerable number of varieties.

ESCALLONIA Any tree or shrub that can be used with advantage as a hedge should do well in most gardens as a specimen. This is certainly true of escallonia, a flowering evergreen that produces its blooms in summer and early autumn, sometimes a dull period in the garden. Bushes are usually 1-3m (3-10ft) in height, normally lime tolerant, capable of standing up to seaside winds and only one or two of the less

Erica carnea

well-known varieties will suffer from frosts. Many of the escallonias were bred by a famous Irish nursery and are now known by its name: Donard Beauty, Donard Brilliance, Donard Gem, Glory of Donard, Pride of Donard and several others, but there are, of course, many other species and varieties suited to our gardens as specimen plants, as hedging materials and as wall plants. Bees love the flowers and although some shrubs may grow large, they can be clipped back after flowering, or if necessary cut right back to old wood.

GARRYA This is an interesting and delightful shrub or small tree which appears to be restricted to one species and even then is grown in far too few gardens. It is difficult to grow, although it is best with a little protection such as might be given by a wall. It is a flowering evergreen, the male and female flowers being borne on separate plants. Garrya is best known for the slender, silky catkins which hang, some 15cm (6in) long, in such profusion that the tree sometimes looks almost like a waterfall. It grows quickly in sun or shade. The only species normally obtainable from most nurseries is the well-known *G. elliptica* and the male form is always sold as opposed to the female which has blackish-brown fruits instead. A variety which might be found in a specialist nursery or might be ordered is *G.e.* 'James Roof'.

Garrya elliptica

Helianthemum nummularium

HEBE These splendid flowering evergreens were once listed under the veronicas. All but one or two originated from New Zealand and have settled down well except that some may not be hardy in colder areas or bleak situations, although they thrive in coastal plantings. They grow well in all soils as long as the drainage is efficient. Flowers are white or various shades of blue. *H. anomala*, growing to about 1m (3ft), with small yellowish-green leaves and white flowers in spikes at the end of summer, is said to be very hardy, as is 'Marjorie', which is a little smaller with white and violet flowers. *H. elliptica* 'Variegata' makes a low shrub with small pale green leaves edged with cream. The violet flowers appear in early summer. This plant should only be grown in milder areas or with added protection.

HELIANTHEMUM The common names sun rose and rock rose indicate that this is a shrub that will glory in a hot sun and a dry site. Nearly all of the available forms have been bred from *H. nummularium*, the common sun rose, and they make wonderful ground-cover plants for sunny sites with poor soil. As a rule the many flowers produced last only a day, but there are so many of them and they are so vivid and spectacular that these plants can bring new beauty to a bare bank, an inaccessible patch or even portions of a rock garden. Look for the 'Ben' varieties, *H. nummularium* 'Ben Dearg', 'Ben Fhada', 'Ben Hope', 'Ben Ledi', 'Ben More' and 'Ben Nevis', all with yellow to deep orange flowers. Creamy-white flowers with a yellow centre are presented by *H.n.* 'The Bride' and rose-crimson with orange centre by 'Watergate Rose'. It really is essential to remember with helianthemums that they must have full sun and a poor soil.

KALMIA Reminiscent of the rhododendron in appearance and in requirements, it is no surprise to find that kalmia is also a member of the Ericaceae. They need an acid soil, preferably moist, and full sun. The leaves are medium to large, oval and a deep, glossy green. It is the flowers that make kalmia distinctive, for they begin as closed buds almost like bladders and then open to become saucer-shaped, usually rose coloured, less frequently red to purple. The species seen to the exclusion of almost any other is *K. latifolia* 'Calico Bush', with rosy pink flowers in large clusters opening in June. There is a variety, *K. l.* 'Clementine Churchill' which is said to be the best of the red-flowered kalmias. *K. angustifolia*, a little smaller, also produces rosy red flowers in June and has the habit of spreading slowly in the garden soil to produce a thicket. It has the common name sheep's laurel. Kalmias must never be allowed to become dry at the roots, so apply mulches of moist peat in spring, particularly in spring droughts.

Kalmia latifolia

MAHONIA Although closely related to the berberis, it is easy to see from the lack of spines and from the compound leaves that this genus is different. Mahonia is nevertheless a useful plant to have in the garden, easy and undemanding, with glossy green leaves and yellow flowers in winter or spring. Known as 'Oregon Grape', *M. aquifolium* grows to a small shrub with leaves that frequently turn scarlet in winter and clustered yellow flowers in early spring followed by blue-black berries. 'Charity' grows rather larger and its deep yellow flowers are to be seen on long racemes almost like spikes in autumn and winter. Another species, *M. japonica*, is one of the most popular plants in our gardens as well as one of the most ornamental, for it has deep green pinnate or divided leaves and long, pendulous, loose racemes of scented lemon-yellow flowers which stay on the plant from late autumn to early spring.

OLEARIA There is something about the daisy bush or tree daisy that proclaims its Australasian origins. The best-known species, *O. haastii*, is very popular. This will grow up to 2m (6ft) tall if it is getting enough sun and can probably be treated as hardy in most parts of northern Europe. It flowers in late summer and when in flower it is sometimes difficult to see the leaves for the blooms. Some of the other species can suffer from sharp frosts when grown inland, although all make remarkably tough barriers against strong winds, excelling near the sea where other plants would suffer burning from the salt-laden winds. The New Zealand holly, *M. macrodonta*, makes a taller tree or shrub, up to 3m (10ft), with long, holly-like leaves silvered beneath and wide panicles of fragrant flowers in June. There are 'Major' and 'Minor' forms. It is worth going quickly over the plant with shears when flowering has finished, a form of dead heading that will ensure the maximum quantity of flowers in the next season.

OSMANTHUS This is a small genus of evergreen shrubs or small trees, with glossy green foliage and beautifully scented little white flowers in spring or autumn. The most popular species is *O. delavayi*, small leaved, growing to about 2m (6ft), with a profusion of small, white, perfumed flowers in April. Another species is *O. burkwoodii*, sometimes *Osmarea burkwoodii* which is the more correct name as it is a rare bi-generic hybrid between *Osmanthus delavayi* and *Phillyrea decora*, raised by the well-known nurserymen Burkwood & Skipwith some 50 years ago. It is hardy, grows to more than 2m (6ft) and produces long, glossy green leaves and fragrant white flowers in April or May. *O. heterophylla* is a species with ten or more useful varieties, mainly slow growing, some bearing shining leaves, often spined like those of a common holly.

Mahonia japonica
Osmarea burkwoodii

PERNETTYA This lovely shrub was named after Antoine Joseph Pernetty, who accompanied Bougainville on his trip to the Falkland Islands in the late eighteenth century. These mainly hardy little shrubs form dense thickets, some dwarf and others taller, producing masses of tiny white flowers to be followed by an abundance of white, pink, red or purple berries, some marbled, all magnificently decorative and largely remaining on the branches through the winter. They grow best in full sun, need a lime-free soil and must be in groups of at least one male to three females to ensure cross-pollination. *P. mucronata* is the best-known species, probably because it is one of the hardiest. It grows to about 50cm (19in) and eventually makes a wonderful ground cover, producing in the meanwhile a froth of white, heath-like flowers in May and June followed by dense clusters of berries coloured from white to purple. There are a number of varieties of this species, some of them with names evocative of the size or colour of the berries produced: Cherry Ripe, Pink Pearl and White Pearl.

PIERIS The pieris, sometimes called andromeda, will grow successfully only where there is no lime and if you garden on limestone the only way to get any success with this wonderful shrub for more than a few months is to grow it on an acid peat hill, which is expensive, or to give it regular doses of chelated

Pernettya mucronata

Pieris taiwanensis

iron, usually known as sequestrene. Although the flower buds are noticeable and attractive throughout the winter, opening as blooms in April and May, white and chalice-shaped, it is the young foliage, red, bronze, white and pink, that is the real glory of the shrub. This young growth is somewhat tender, so protect it with light shade from above and from north and east winds. It is difficult to choose a species for recommendation as there are many that are beautiful. *P.* 'Forest Flame' is fairly hardy and the young foliage appears first as a vivid red, going through pink and then creamy-white before becoming green. The white flowers are in long, drooping pannicles. Another fairly hardy form is *P. japonica* 'Variegata', medium sized, slow growing, with creamy-white young leaves flushed with pale pink.

PYRACANTHA The firethorn tells all in the name, for the masses of red, orange or yellow berries can certainly give the impression of fire and the stems are thorny or spined, a fact which differentiates it from the rather similar cotoneaster. Bushes are often grown against a wall or fence, where they certainly show to advantage, but they can be grown as single specimens. Their main impact is through the berries in autumn and winter rather than the summer flowers which are of lesser significance. Plants grow easily, are completely hardy, adapt to any soil and are tolerant of polluted air. The best known and most frequently grown variety is *P. coccinea* 'Lalandei', strong and upright, covered in orange fruits in autumn.

SANTOLINA The cotton lavender, santolina, makes a low mound of silvery-grey foliage which in July raises tall stems topped with pretty yellow button flowers. It likes full sun and a well-drained soil. A dwarf species that has proved popular over the years is *S. chamaecyparissus*, which grows to about 50cm (19in) tall and has finely divided leaves which appear to be covered with a soft, silver wool, highly aromatic when crushed in the fingers. An even smaller, more compact variety is *S.c. corsica*, sometimes known as 'Nana', suitable for the rock garden but apt to be lost, perhaps, if grown with full-sized shrubs or herbaceous material.

SENECIO This is one of the comparatively few shrubby members of the enormous family Compositae, the daisy family, but it is probably true to say that it is grown more for its silver grey, soft and silky foliage than for the daisy flowers, usually yellow, which appear in June. *S. greyi* and *S. laxifolius* are the most frequently seen species and few gardeners other than botanical experts would be able to say with certainty which

Senecio greyi

Skimmia japonica

was which. Both are evergreen, growing to about 1m (3ft) with silvery, downy leaves when young, turning greener and tougher when more mature. Flowers are yellow. These two species are said to be hardy, but most others are not and it might be wise to give a little protection to plants when frosts threaten. Several of the species are recommended only for the mildest parts of this country, although curiously enough almost all senecios are said to withstand sea breezes and one, *S. reinoldii*, is claimed to be one of the best shrubs for windswept gardens by the sea; it will take the full blast of the Atlantic Ocean.

SKIMMIA A small genus of little, compact shrubs, domed, neat, tolerant of shade and excellent for both industrial and coastal areas. Both male and female plants are necessary if you wish to enjoy the handsome, glistening, scarlet fruits throughout the whole of the winter months. *S. japonica* is the best species, growing well in both chalky and acid soils and its variety, *S.j.* 'Foremanii' is a strongly growing female clone which carries large bunches of the brilliant red berries. *S.j.* 'Fragrans' is the male, with dense panicles of white flowers which have a pleasant perfume rather like lilies-of-the-valley. There is a hermaphrodite form, *S. reevesiana*, which makes a dwarf shrub less than 1m (3ft) tall and with leaves which sometimes have a pale, silvery margin. The white flowers appear in May, followed by dull crimson fruits which last through the winter and are often still on the branches when the flowers begin to appear again in the following May. This species demands an acid soil.

DECIDUOUS SHRUBS

CEANOTHUS Nearly all the many species and varieties of ceanothus came originally from California, hence 'Californian lilac', and most of them show clearly that they prefer the Californian climate to that in Europe. Ceanothus is divided into two groups, the evergreen and the deciduous. The deciduous species are a little tougher and have larger leaves and looser clusters of the famous blue flowers. *C.* 'Gloire de Versailles', with its large panicles of powder-blue flowers in summer and autumn, is one of the best blue-flowered shrubs for gardens. Another good one from the same group is *C.* 'Topaz', summer flowering, with light indigo-blue flowers. All plants like the full sun and a well-drained soil which can even contain a little lime. Deciduous ceanothus can be cut back to within 15cm (6in) of the previous year's growth in about February or March. Some species have white or pink flowers and of these the pink *C.* 'Marie Simon' is to be recommended.

CHAENOMELES The popularity of this shrub is indicated by the number of its names. It is called cydonia or japonica and its fruit is quince. It is easy to grow, tolerant of

Chaenomeles superba

any soil and situation. It will grow well against a wall or fence and as a specimen or in a border, producing large, saucer-shaped flowers, red, orange and white in spring, to be followed by large yellow quinces. The most numerous and probably the best of the quinces originate with two species, *C. speciosa* and *C. superba*, each of which provides us with 20 or so good varieties. Among varieties of *C. speciosa* we find, for example, 'Cardinalis', crimson scarlet; 'Phylis Moore', almond-pink, semi-double; 'Rubra grandiflora', with low, sprawling habit, crimson and extra large; and 'Simonii', blood-red, flat, semi-double, with a dwarf habit. And among the *C. superba* varieties, slightly smaller but very vigorous, perhaps the best is 'Knap Hill Scarlet'.

CHIMONANTHUS There is less choice here, for this genus has only one species, *C. praecox*. The winter sweet, as it is popularly known, is a favourite because its flowers are so sweetly perfumed and appear on the plants in winter before the leaves. It makes a medium-size shrub which grows well in any type of soil including chalk. It will grow as a specimen or in a border, but does best with the protection of a wall, which helps to ripen the wood for the production of the flowers. *C. praecox* takes a little while to produce its pale, waxy, yellow flowers, purple stained in the centre, but once started it will flower every year. *C.p.* 'Grandiflorus' has deeper yellow flowers stained with red and *C.p.* 'Luteus' has larger blooms.

Chimonanthus praecox

CORYLOPSIS A relative of the witch hazel, corylopsis is neither as well known nor as frequently grown as it deserves. It is easy and tolerant, though perhaps a little susceptible to frost damage and so requiring a certain amount of shelter or protection during winter. The hanging racemes of fragrant yellow flowers appear before the leaves in early spring. A good species is *C. pauciflora*, which will grow to about 2m (6ft) in time, with large leaves, pink when newly unfolding, and early primrose-yellow scented flowers. More upright growing is *C. veitchiana*, which has large racemes of flowers, primrose-yellow again but with noticeably brick-red anthers. One of the tallest is *C. willmottiae* which can reach 3m (10ft). It has erect branches and the tassels of yellow flowers are 7cm (3in) long with a strong scent.

DAPHNE Small shrubs with perfumed flowers, white, pink to purple, these are sometimes difficult to establish in the garden, needing a good loamy soil, moisture at the roots and a site in the sun or perhaps the lightest of shade. There are a number of species, among which is *D. cneorum*, dwarf, about 50cm (19in), known as the garland flower because of the clusters of fragrant rose-pink blooms that appear on the branches in spring. There are several varieties, two of which, *D.c.* 'Eximia' and *D.c.* 'Pygmaea', are prostrate, with branches growing flat on the soil. Called by some the 'mezereon', a little taller and a little easier to grow, *D. mezereum* flowers in February and March, with purple-red flowers. It will grow in chalk. Among its varieties are *D.m.* 'Alba', with white flowers; *D.m.* 'Grandiflora' with larger flowers beginning to open in autumn and *D.m.* 'Rosea' with large, rose-pink blooms. *D. odora* 'Aureo marginata' is a hardy form, much appreciated for its sweet perfume in winter. It needs a sunny, sheltered position. Because daphne transplant badly, it is wise to buy container-grown plants.

DEUTZIA A rich source of small, decorative, easily grown flowering shrubs with a wide choice of modern varieties, most of these grow no more than 2m (6ft) tall and all are clothed in neat green leaves and abundantly decorated with white to pink and purple flowers. *D.* 'Magicien', with large mauve-pink flowers edged with white and with purple undersides is worth growing, as is *D. longiflora* 'Veitchii', with its large clusters of lilac-pink flowers in June and July. A larger, taller form is presented by *D. scabra* and its varieties *D.s.* 'Candidissima', with double flowers, pure white, and *D.s.* 'Macrocephala' has large white bell-shaped flowers. It is helpful with the deutzias to thin out and cut right back all flowering shoots almost to the old wood immediately after they have bloomed. *D. rosea* has broad white or pink blooms.

Daphne odora 'Aureo marginata'
Deutzia rosea

HAMAMELIS The witch hazels are much loved, mainly because of the strongly perfumed flowers that brave the winter cold and appear on bare branches from December through to about March. The curious shape of the slim petals can produce flowers which measure between 2-3 cm (½-1in) across. Best of all the witch hazels are those from China, *H. mollis*, making large shrubs with clusters of great golden-yellow, sweetly perfumed, wide-petalled flowers from December to March. The large, round, hairy leaves turn an attractive yellow in autumn. There are a number of varieties, all with large, strongly scented flowers, most of them tinged with red or orange. The exception is *H. mollis* 'Pallida', which has sulphur-yellow flowers, sweetly and strongly scented, crowded in clusters along the naked stems. In autumn the shrub turns yellow. Plants prefer an acid soil and like to be in sun or light shade.

PHILADELPHUS Called mock orange, possibly because of the perfume, and also erroneously called syringa, this nevertheless remains one of our finest garden shrubs because it gives a marvellous performance with the least possible demands. It will grow in any soil under any conditions, yet grown under good conditions in a spot with space, good soil, plenty of sun and air, it will perform like the star it undoubtedly is. The June and July flowers are normally white and strongly perfumed. The shrub grows between 1-2m (3-6ft) under

Philadelphus erectus

normal conditions. One species, *P. coronarius*, a small shrub with creamy-white perfumed flowers, is said to be particularly easy to grow on dry soils. Of its two varieties, *P.c.* 'Aureus' has bright yellow leaves when young and those of *P.c.* 'Variegatus' have a creamy-white margin. *P.* 'Erectus' is an upright shrub, highly floriferous and richly scented. Smaller, more compact, growing to less than 1m (3ft), is *P.* 'Manteau d'Hermine' with fragrant, creamy-white double flowers, while much the same size is *P.* 'Sybille', with single, almost square purple-stained, orange-scented blooms. But perhaps the best double flowered cultivar is still *P.* 'Virginal', growing to nearly 3m (10ft), bearing heavily perfumed flowers a full 5cm (2in) across.

POTENTILLA Hardy, growing easily in any soil, accepting sun or light shade, the potentilla produces flowers like small, single, white or orange-yellow roses, sometimes beginning in June and sometimes ending in November. The main species is *P. fruticosa* and there are so many varieties that it is difficult to recommend choices, but among those that have achieved awards are the following: *P.f.* 'Grandiflora' with large, canary yellow flowers; *P.f.* 'Katherine Dykes', primrose-yellow flowers; *P.f.* 'Mandshurica', dwarf, low-growing, white flowers; *P.f.* 'Harviflora', with an abundance of yellow flowers; and *P.f.* 'Vilmoriniana', erect, up to 2m (6ft), with silvery leaves and creamy flowers.

Potentilla fruticosa

Rhus typhina 'Laciniata'

PRUNUS The prunus family is so heavily represented among the flowering trees that it is surprising to find riches in the shrubby section, all moderately easy to grow and flourishing in sun or light shade on most garden soils. Among the deciduous species there is the interesting and rewarding dwarf Russian almond, about 1m (3ft) tall, making little thickets of slim stems, advancing by suckers, producing saw-toothed leaves and semi-double red flowers in April. This is *P. tenella* 'Fire Hill' and it likes to be planted in full sun. *P. glandulosa* 'Albiplena' again makes a rounded and twiggy bush 1m (3ft) tall, but in this case with a mass of miniature double white flowers. Exactly the same but with tiny bright pink flowers is *P.g.* 'Sinensis'. *P. triloba* 'Multiplex' grows quite differently as a broad shrub nearly 2m (6ft) tall, producing its double pink flowers in March before the leaves open.

RHUS Known as the stag's horn sumach from the almost furry terminal sections of the branching stems, rhus is grown mainly for its foliage, a rich and glowing orange and red in autumn. The flowers are insignificant but in some species these are followed by fruits of the female plants, crimson and small. *R. typhina* is the species most frequently grown and this makes a wide, spreading shrub with thick branches covered at the tips with reddish-brown hairs. Green clusters of flowers appear on the male plant and smaller groups on the female (*Rhus typhina* 'Laciniata') which also bears the dense, conical clusters of hairy red fruits. This rhus is invasive and will send up suckers in the soil around the area in which it grows. These suckers can be separated and used as new plants, they can be cut down to ground level, or they can be killed chemically, but should not just be ignored unless a whole thicket is required. Branches are best pruned almost to the ground in February.

RIBES This group of spring-flowering shrubs appears to be known only from *R. sanguineum*, the popular flowering currant, which is a pity, for there are others that are well worth growing, such as *R. odoratum*, the buffalo currant, smallish, erect, with shining green leaves which colour dramatically in autumn. Loose racemes of golden yellow flowers, clove scented, appear in April, followed by black berries. There is also *R. speciosum* from California, which produces clusters of rich, red blooms almost like fuchsias in April and May. This species is perhaps slightly tender and could do with some protection. The flowering currant itself, *R. sanguineum*, is a medium-sized shrub with flowers from white to a deep crimson, single or double. Plants will grow in any soil, in sun or shade, and it is helpful to cut back shoots after flowering.

Ribes sanguineum

SPIREA This is a quick-growing, wide-ranging shrub that is easy to grow under almost any circumstances and will perform with grace and beauty in the shrub border, as a specimen or even as a hedge. Generally the spring-flowering types produce white flowers and the summer-flowering pink to red. To keep performance at its best, cut out weak and old stems of the spring-flowering types when the flowers have faded and prune the summer-flowering varieties in about March almost down to ground level. Best known of the spring-flowering types is probably *S. arguta*, called bridal wreath and foam of May, medium-sized, dense growing, with snow-white flowers in small clusters all along the stems in April and May. There is also *S. nipponica* 'Snowmound', which does indeed make a mound about 50cm (19in) tall, with small white flowers smothering the branches. In the summer-flowering group look for *S. bumalda* 'Anthony Waterer', which makes a low, twiggy shrub with upright stems reaching nearly 1m (3ft). The flowers form large, flat clusters made up of many tiny carmine flowers opening in July to September.

VIBURNUM A large and highly rewarding genus of shrubs which can be used in several ways in the garden. All are hardy, easy to grow and will flourish in almost any soil. For convenience they can be divided into three separate groups: those that bloom in winter, the spring-flowering group and

Spirea bumalda

those that are grown for their berries or winter leaf colour. Earliest to flower is *V. farreri* (previously known as *V. fragrans*) which opens its pale pink buds in November to produce tight clusters of perfumed white flowers which go on to February, although even this is beaten sometimes by *V. bodnantense*, which in a helpful season can produce larger flowers earlier and longer lasting. In the spring-flowering group *V. carlesii* makes a neat, rounded, medium-sized bush with white flowers, sweetly scented. The popular snowball tree, *V. opulus* 'Sterile', makes a dense shrub about 2m (6ft) tall and wide; its snowball flowers appear first as a small, tight, green ball and then open to its familiar size and colour. 'Grandiflorum' is rather larger. Two indigenous members bring autumn colour. They are *V. lantana*, the wayfaring tree, with white flowers in June followed by red berries turning black, and *V. opulus*, the Guelder rose, again having white flowers in June but with red berries and vivid orange and red foliage.

WEIGELA A small shrub which will make itself at home almost anywhere but needs a good, rich soil. The abundant flowers appear mainly in June, usually in tones of reds and pinks. The best form is probably *W. florida* 'Variegata', slow growing to just over 1m (3ft), with pretty green leaves variegated with creamy-yellow margins and with pale pink perfumed flowers. Prune all plants right back in winter.

Viburnum juddii

PLANTS FOR HEDGING

BERBERIS If you decide to use berberis as a hedging material a considerable choice is open to you. You can have evergreen or deciduous, flowered, berried, tall or short. An informal, low-growing hedge, deciduous, with interesting foliage, is provided by *B. thunbergii* 'Atropurpurea nana', neat and compact, with reddish-purple leaves, growing to about 50cm (19in). Plant 30cm (12in) apart and trim in winter. If you prefer a green hedge try the deciduous *B. verruculosa*, slow growing to more than 1m (3ft), with small, dark green leaves, white beneath, and golden yellow flowers. For more normal hedging heights the berberis is still useful. *B. stenophylla*, evergreen, will grow 2-3m (6-9ft), with sprays of yellow flowers in May and June if left untrimmed (normally done after flowering) and berries in autumn. Plant about 60cm (24in) apart. *P. darwinii* will provide orange-yellow flowers from April to May and, unpruned, purple berries. Plant 60cm (24in) apart. Or try *B. panlanensis*, a neat green species. These three taller growing species are all evergreen.

CARPINUS The hornbeam can make an excellent hedge and is treated very much like an ordinary beech hedge. The common hornbeam, *Carpinus betulus*, is the best species for a hedge, making a medium to large tree with ribbed and toothed leaves which, like beech, will hang onto the branches during much of the winter if the tree is trimmed in August. It does not make as strong a hedge as beech, so under some conditions it is grown with thorn, one hornbeam to six quickthorns, where a strong barrier is required to keep out farm animals. Hornbeams are suitable for clay or chalky soils, even when wet. The variety *C.b.* 'Fastigiata' is also suitable for a hedge, slim at first but spreading out after it has been growing for a year or two.

CHAMAECYPARIS Blue-grey *Chamaecyparis lawsoniana* 'Allumii' and *C.l.* 'Fletcheri', slow growing, both make good, solid, formal hedges of about 2m (6ft) and should be planted about 60cm (24in) apart. *C.l.* 'Green Hedger', with rich green foliage, as its name suggests was specially bred as a hedging plant and has proved highly successful. *C.l.* 'Lutea' has golden foliage, as has *C.l. pisifera* 'Plumosa aurea', with a softer, more feathery texture. Do not let these hedges grow too rapidly to their required height, but trim them very lightly three or four times in the first year or two to encourage strong growth near the base and after this give a single annual trim.

Berberis thunbergii 'Atropurpurea'

FAGUS The beech provides us with some of our greatest and most noble trees as well as suitable forms for attractive hedges. A well-grown, tall beech hedge in spring shows to greatest advantage the soft green foliage which later turns darker and hangs, crisp brown, rustling, on the branches until pushed off by the new growth in the next spring. The most attractive way to grow a beech hedge is to plant one purple-leaved variety to every ten of the green, depending upon personal taste. In winter no real difference can be seen. The common beech, *F. sylvatica*, is the species to use for a hedge and the purple-leaved variety is *F.s.* 'Purpurea'. Plant both kinds about 50cm (20in) apart, preferably in staggered rows about 20cm (8in) apart. Try not to allow growth to exceed 15cm (6in) a year, but do not be afraid of cutting right back into old wood if too much space is being stolen.

FUCHSIA These make a most glamorous and exciting hedge if the climate is suitable, though as a general rule only gardens in the warmer southern areas provide conditions in which fuchsia hedges can flourish. Because plants are liable to damage from early frosts, it is helpful to put them into the soil with the base of the shoots about 10cm (4in) below ground level. Plant 45-60cm (18-24in) apart in May and trim in spring by cutting back lightly if there has been little or no frost damage during the winter and more severely if there has, even almost down to ground level. *F. magellanica* and its varieties are the best and toughest plants to use for hedging. This has long, slim flowers, with scarlet calyx and violet petals. The variety *F.m.* 'Alba' has shorter, white flowers. *F.m.* 'Pumila' is a dwarf type with tiny scarlet and violet flowers. *F.* 'Riccartonii' is quite often seen as a hedge in milder districts, usually picked out by its deeper coloured calyx and broader petals. The best florist fuchsia for hedging is probably 'Mrs. Popple', small, large-flowered, almost hardy, with dramatic scarlet sepals, violet petals and long crimson stamens and style.

LONICERA The shrubby honeysuckles are quite different from the climbing kinds. They are quick growing in any ordinary soil, not as hardy as privet but neater and denser. *Lonicera nitida*, the Chinese honeysuckle, makes a particularly compact hedge because it grows densely and because it can be trimmed into accurate lines and angles. The best form is *L.n.* 'Fertilis', strong growing, erect, with long, arching branchlets and neat foliage. It should be planted about 30cm (12in) apart and can be allowed to grow to about 1.5m (5ft) tall. Cut back after planting to within 25-30cm (10-12in) of the soil. Trimming should take place twice a year in April and August. A colourful variety is *L.n.* 'Baggesen's Gold', which has yellow leaves.

Thuja plicata

PRUNUS Besides the flowering cherries, almonds and the like, the prunus family produces some excellent shrubby hedging material of a dwarf and tougher nature. Myrobalan plum, *P. cerasifera*, has long been used as a country hedge, planted in winter, trimmed in July or August. There are also *P.c.* 'Pissardii' and 'Nigra' both excellent hedging material.

ROSA Roses can make a good informal hedge but need plenty of space if they are to be practical enough to serve as a useful barrier to animals as well as humans. The modern hybrids do not make a good hedge by themselves and some of the old-fashioned roses, *Rosa rugosa*, the shrub roses and the hybrid musks are the most useful. Zephirine Drouhin, the thornless rose, flowering from early June, makes a fragrant hedge up to 4m (13ft) tall. *R. eglanteria*, the sweet briar, sometimes known as *R. rubiginosa*, produces single pink flowers. Make sure all roses are planted in good soil that has

Old English Rose

been well dug and cleared of all weeds. If you can, incorporate plenty of farmyard manure or rich compost in the trench before planting.

THUJA A small genus of hardy evergreen trees and shrubs among which are one or two subjects which make first-class hedging material. The most strongly recommended species is *T. plicata*, also known as western red cedar, which normally makes a large, quick-growing timber tree. The variety 'Atrovirens' has bright green foliage and is best planted 60cm (24in) apart. *T. occidentalis*, greenish-leaved in summer, turns brownish-green in winter. Plant 45-60cm (18-24in) apart in late September or October or in March or April. Try to get plants about 50-60cm (20-24in) tall. Larger plants may be used for a hedge but will grow more slowly than smaller, younger specimens. Trim frequently while young, but leave the top until it reaches the required height.

CLIMBERS

CLEMATIS A wide-ranging genus of evergreen and deciduous flowering and climbing shrubs, all of which can climb only with assistance from trellis, wire or some other support. They can be in flower from April to October. Most clematis are deciduous and very hardy, although the evergreens generally need a little protection. The species and small flowered cultivars begin the season in April with *C. macropetala*, followed by *C. montana*, most vigorous of all clematis, with white, vanilla-scented flowers. The purples and pinks of *C. viticella* and relatives arrive in June. The large flowered hybrids with 'Nelly Moser' type blooms dazzle us in May and June to be followed by the main display of the Jackmanii group. Clematis pruning, which appears to be complex, can be reduced to the rules that the *C. montana* group should be lightly thinned after flowering, *C.* Jackmanii type should be cut right back to within 30cm (12in) of the soil in February and the others should merely be thinned and shortened slightly at much the same time.

Clematis 'Nelly Moser'

Hedera colchica

HEDERA Ivies grow in any soil, they tolerate sun and shade, they are hardy, they climb by themselves with no support, they may be pruned lightly or severely and will continue to grow happily. There are few species but many varieties, differing in size and colour of leaf and to some extent in habit of growth. Some of the varieties differ slightly according to the conditions under which they grow. The common ivy is *Hedera helix*. Others include *H. canariensis*, variegated cream; and *H. colchica*, with large dark green leaves.

LONICERA Honeysuckles will grow in almost any soil, will flower happily in sun or shade and given a minimum of support or assistance will climb and scramble over almost anything in their path. Still the best species in many ways is the woodbine, the common wild honeysuckle of country hedges, *L. periclymenum*, with flowers some 5cm (2in) long, strongly and sweetly perfumed, creamy-white within and purplish or yellowish outside, flowering from June to September and followed by shining red berries. *L. sempervirens* is evergreen, a rich orange-scarlet outside and yellow within, 4-5cm (1½-2in) long.

PARTHENOCISSUS Strong, partially self-clinging by means of little suction pads on the tendrils, these vines will grow under most conditions and climb a wall or a tree, producing foliage of unique, glossy green in spring and dazzling red, orange and yellow in autumn. *P. quinquefolia* is the original Virginia creeper, now believed to be surpassed by *P. henryana*, with its particularly beautiful foliage.

VITIS These vines, normally grown for decorative purposes, will produce only token fruits as a rule, although *V. vinifera* 'Brandt' can deliver small bunches, almost cylindrical, of edible fruit in some seasons. These climbers use strong, wiry tendrils to pull themselves along and upwards, so they must have some support on which to climb.

WISTERIA A small family of deciduous climbing plants, they are known and loved for the long racemes of white, blue, purple or pink flowers produced in May and June. Vines should grow in full sun and when growing strongly may require an annual drastic pruning in late winter plus an August shortening of the main shoots. The Chinese wisteria, *W. sinensis*, is the most popular species.

Vitis vinifera 'Brandt'

INDEX

Numbers in italics refer to illustrations

Abelia spp. 62
A. chinensis 'Frances Mason' 42
Acer spp. 50
A. campestre 10, 50
A. griseum 48
A. japonicum 'Aureum' 42
A. palmatum *43*, 50
A. platanoides 4, 50
aftercare 28-9
Amelanchier spp. 49, 50-1
A. canadensis *50*, 51
Arbutus 14, 49
A. unedo 'Rubra' *49*
ash, flowering 46-7
Aucuba japonica 22
azaleas 14, 17
Azara microphylla 47

bark and wood 48, 49
bay tree 46
beech 10, 15, 42, 88
Berberis spp. 10, 15, 49, 62, 86
B. darwinii 62, 86
B. lologensis *63*
B. stenophylla 62, 86
B. thunbergii 'Atropurpurea' 86, *87*
Betula papyrifera 48
B. pendula 'Youngii' 9, *9*
bonemeal 26, 30
box 39
buddleia 39, 47
buying plants 36-7

cacti 24
Californian lilac 76
Callicarpa bodinieri 49
Calluna 62
C. vulgaris 62, *63*
Camellia 15, 21, 22, 40, 64
C. japonica *23*, 64
C. williamsii *64*
Carpenteria californica 9
Carpinus 86
C. betulus 86
Catalpa bignonioides 'Aurea' 42
caterpillars 32
Ceanothus spp. 39, 76
Cercis siliquastrum 51, *51*
Chaenomeles spp. 76-7
C. superba *76* 77
Chamaecyparis spp. 58, 86
C. lawsoniana *11*, 42, 58, 86
C. nootkatensis 'Pendula' 9
cherry, flowering 15, 32, 46, 54, 90
Chimonanthus praecox 47, *77*, 77-8
Chinese honeysuckle 88
Chinese wisteria 94
chlorisis 32
choisya 15
Christmas tree 60
cistus 38, 46
Clematis spp. 18, 92
C. flammula 18
C. 'Nelly Moser' 92, *92*
climate 20-1
climbers 18, 92-4
coloured and variegated plants 42
Colutea arborescens 49
compost, homemade 24
compost bins *29*
conifers 4, 17, *20* 44-5, 58-61
container-grown plants:
buying 36, *37*
planting 27
containers, trees and shrubs in 17
Convolvulus cneorum 17
Cornus 39
C. alba 'Sibirica' 48, *48*
C. kousa chinensis 9
Corylopsis spp. 78
Corylus maxima 'Purpurea' 49
crab, flowering 46, 48, 54
Cotoneaster spp. 10, 13, 49, 52, 64-5
C. horizontalis 52, *52* 65
Crataegus spp. 52-3
Cupressocyparis 10, 58
Cupressus spp. 10, 58
C. arizonica 'Bonita' *59*
currant, flowering 83
cuttings 38-9
cytisus 39

daisy bush 70
Daphne spp. 47, 78
D. odora 'Aureo marginata' 78, *79*
deciduous shrubs 4, 76-85
Deutzia spp. 78
D. rosea *79*
disease and pest control 32-3
division 40, *41*
drought 20

Elaeagnus spp. 65
E. pungens 65, *65*
Epimedium perralderianum 13
Erica spp. 13, 15, 32, 40, 66
E. carnea 66, *66*
Escallonia 66-7
eucalyptus trees 46
euonymus 42
evergreen shrubs 4, 62-75

Fagus 88
F. sylvatica 9, *11* 88
Fatsia japonica 17
fertilizers 24, 26, 29, 30
forsythia 39, 40
Fraxinus ornus 46-7
frost 20-1, 39
fruits and berries 48-9
Fuchsia 15, 88
F. magellanica 88

Garrya 67
G. elliptica *67*
Gaultheria procumbens 49
genista 38
Gleditschia triacanthos 48
grafting 40
ground cover, shrubs as 12-13
Guelder rose 85

habit and rate of growth 44-5
Hamamelis spp. 80
H. mollis 47, 80
hawthorn or may 15, 32, 52-3
heather 62, 66
Hebe spp. 68
Hedera spp. 93
H. colchica 93, *93*
hedges 10
cutting back 30-1
planting 30-1
plants for 86-91
Helianthemum 68
H. nummularium 68, *68*
holly 15, 42, 49
honeysuckle 18, 39, 40, 47, 88, 93-4
hormone powder 39
hornbeam 10, 86
horse chestnut 48
humus 24
hydrangeas 15, 39
Hypericum calycinum 12, *13*

ivies 12, 13, 18, 93

Japanese cherries 54
Japanese laurel 22
Japanese maple 50
japonica 77
jasmine 18, 47
John Innes composts 24
June berry 51
Juniperus spp. 60
J. sabina *12*
J. virginiana 'Skyrocket' 4, 60

Kalmia spp. 69
K. latifolia 69, *69*
kerria 40
Koelreuteria spp. 53
K. paniculata 48, 53

laburnum 32
larch 15
laurels 22, 54
Laurus 39
L. nobilis 46
laurustinus, winter-flowering 22
Lavandula spica 46
lavender 46, 47
Lawson cypress 58
layering 40, *41*
lilacs 4, 40
limes 47
Liriodendron tulipifera 9
L. t. 'Aureo marginatum' 42
Lonicera spp. 88, 93-4

Magnolia stellata 8
Mahonia 47, 70
M. aquifolium 13, 70
M. japonica 22, 70, *71*
Malus spp. 54
M. floribunda 55
manure, farmyard 24, 28, 30
manna 46
maples 4, 50
common or field 10, 50
variegated 42
Metasequoia glyptostroboides 9
mixed shrub border 6-7
mock orange 80
Monterey cypress 58
Morus spp. 54
M. nigra 48, 54
mulberries 48, 54
mulches 20, 28, 29
myrobalan plum 10, 90
myrtle 47

New Zealand holly 70
Norway maple 50

Olearia spp. 70
Oregon grape 13
ornamental fruits, bark and wood 48-9
Osmanthus spp. 70
O. burkwoodii 70, *71*
O. decora 49
Osmarea burkwoodii 70, *71*

pachysandra 40
Parrotia persica 9
Parthenocissus spp. 94
passion fruit 18
peach leaf curl 32, 54
peach trees 54
pear, decorative 56
peat 32
periwinkles 12, 15
Pernettya spp. 72
P. mucronata 72, *72*
Pfitzer juniper 60
Philadelphus 39, *46*, 80-1
P. erectus 80, 81
phlomis 15
Phormium 42
P. tenax 17
Picea spp. 60
P. pungens 61
Pieris spp. 15, 72-3
P. taiwanensis 73
pinus 10
planting:
aftercare 28-9
bare root trees 26-7
container-grown trees 27
hedge 30-1
Polygonum baldschuanicum 18
poplars 42
Populus balsamifera 46
P. candicans 'Aurora' 42
Portugal laurel 22, 54
Potentilla spp. 38, 81
P. fruticosa 19, 81, *81*
pre-packed plants, buying 36
privet 10
pruning 34-5
Prunus spp. 22, 54, 82, 90
P. cerasifera 'Pissardii' 54, 90
Pyracantha spp. 10, 49, 73
P. crenulata 23
Pyrus spp. 56
P. salicifolia 'Pendula' 56, *56*

quickthorn 10
quince 18, 49, 77

Rhamnus frangula 49
Rhododendron ponticum 10
rhododendrons 10, 15, 17, 24, 32, 40, *41*
Rhus spp. 40, 82-3
R. typhina 'Laciniata' *82*, 83
Ribes spp. 83
R. sanguineum 83, *83*
Robinia pseudoacacia 'Frisia' 9, 42
Rosa spp. roses 10, 18, 46, 90-1
Old English *90*
species 15, 47
Rose of Sharon 12
rosemary 46
Ruscus aculeatus 49
Russian almond 82
Russian vine 18

Salix spp. 56-7
S. alba 'Chermesina' 9
S. 'Caerulea' 57
S. caprea 'Pendula' *25*
S. daphnoides 57, *57*
Salvia officinalis 46
Santolina spp. 74
S. chamaecyparissus 74
scented flowers and aromatic foliage 46-7
seeds, raising plants from 38
Senecio spp. 74-5
S. greyi 74, *74*
sequestrene 72-3
silver leaf 32
Skimmia spp. 49, 75
S. japonica 75, *75*
snowball tree 85
snowfalls *20* 31
Snowy mespilus 51
soil and drainage 24
Sorbus spp. 15, 57
S. esserteauana 46
Spartium junceum 47
specimen trees, planting 8-9
Spirea spp. 39, 84
S. bumalda 84, *84*
stag's horn sumach 82
strawberry tree 49
sun and shade 22
sycamores 50
Symphoricarpus 49
Syringa vulgaris 'Maud Notcutt' 4
systemic insecticides/ pesticides 32, 33

Taxus 60
T. baccata 9, 60
Thuja 10, 91
T. plicata 89, 91
thymes 13
tilias (limes) 47
training trees and shrubs 34-5
tulip tree 9, 42

Viburnum spp. 39, 49, 84-5
V. farreri (*V. fragrans*) 47, 85
V. juddii 85
V. tinus 22
Virginia creeper 18
Vitis (vines) 49, 94
V. vinifera 'Brandt' 94, *94*

wall and climbing shrubs 18
wayfaring tree 85
Weigela 39, 85
western red cedar 91
willows 24, 32, 39, 56-7
Kilmarnock *25*
weeping 56-7
wintersweet 47
Wisteria 94
witch hazel 46, 47, 78, 80
woodland garden 14-15

yews 10, 60
yucca 42